Jeannie Vanasco is the highly acclaimed author of *My Father's Glass Eye*. Her writing has appeared in the *Times Literary Supplement*, *The New York Times*, and the *New Yorker*. She lives in Baltimore where she works as an Assistant Professor of English at Towson University.

'With matchless grit and a vibrant mind, Jeannie Vanasco performs an absorbing autopsy on a friendship that ended in rape. *Things We Didn't Talk About When I Was a Girl* cuts through the silence of deep betrayal, gives contour to the aching space between forgiveness and absolution, and offers a living testament to the endless wreckage of sexual assault.'

Amy Jo Burns, author of *Cinderland*

'Unflinching in her honesty and approach, Vanasco interrogates boundaries further shaping and re-shaping memoir as we know it. Wickedly clever and powerful, *this* is a necessary book.'

Krystal A. Sital, author of
Secrets We Kept: Three Women of Trinidad

'Jeannie Vanasco's rigorous and nuanced investigation of crime, trauma, secrets, and the telling of our stories, applies an agile mind and penetrating insight to the enforced silences that surround rape and its aftermath.'

Lisa Locascio, author of *Open Me*

'In this brave and urgent memoir, Jeannie Vanasco asks if it's possible for a good person to commit a terrible act. In a moment where morality is so often rendered in flat, simplistic terms, Vanasco refuses to take the easy way out: she is generous yet exacting, fair yet relentless. A searching, brilliant book and Jeannie Vanasco is a formidable talent.'

Daniel Gumbiner, *The Boatbuilder*

'Explores the common experience of rape with uncommon nuance and intense tenderness. In the process, the book also unexpectedly becomes a warm celebration of female friendship. Vanasco reveals the boundaries of your thoughts and feelings. Then she takes you beyond.'

YZ Chin, author of *Though I Get Home*

'Vanasc   rapist,
questio   rs into

Windsor and Maidenhead

9580000122668

her processing of that experience is, frankly, stunning. This is a book I'll teach and reread well into the future, grateful that fewer and fewer girls will grow up without the opportunity to talk about these things.'

Angela Pelster, author of *Limber*

'A work of astounding control, able to reach places I never expected a book to reach. It is both a conversation between Jeannie Vanasco and her former friend, Mark, and a conversation between Vanasco and herself—about paradox and betrayal, owing and being owed, and the complex terminology of sexual violence. Vanasco writes not just about whether it is possible to be 'a good person who commits a terrible act,' but about having to consider the weight of the word good. It has left me transfixed.'

Thomas Mira Y Lopez, author of *The Book of Resting Places*

'A compelling and courageous memoir, and I salute Jeannie Vanasco for refusing to write in clichés about her teenage trauma. Anyone can look at a rapist and see a monster, but she insists on seeing a human being instead. This book is a timely reminder that rigorous thinking, empathy and the desire to understand are always right, never wrong. It was an absolute honour to read Jeannie's book.'

Elizabeth Brooks, author of *Call of the Curlew*

'A thoughtful, conflicted, harrowing examination of what Mark did - with his words alongside her own... Clearly this is an important and timely book... heartfelt, painful and essential.'

Shelf Awareness

'There is so much power in these pages: in the vulnerability she shows in seeking answers, in the deftness with which she builds a narrative where there was once only a mess of questions and silence.'

Elissa Washuta, author of *My Body Is a Book of Rules*

THINGS WE DIDN'T TALK ABOUT WHEN I WAS A GIRL

JEANNIE VANASCO

DUCKWORTH

This edition first published in the United Kingdom by
Duckworth in 2019

Duckworth, an imprint of Prelude Books ltd
13 Carrington Road, Richmond
TW10 5AA United Kingdom
www.preludebooks.co.uk

For bulk and special sales please contact
info@preludebooks.co.uk

A catalogue record for this book is available from the
British Library

Text design and Typesetting by Geethik Technologies

Printed and bound in Great Britain by Clays

9780715653753

For Hannah

But what is the word for what I experienced after?

From *Nightingale: A Gloss*
by PAISLEY REKDAL

Early evening. We were in your car, at the end of your block, at a stop sign. The streets were empty. My window was open because I hated closed windows—probably because I thought my *why drive if you can't feel the wind* attitude made me profound. We were sixteen.

I just needed to leave my house, you said.

With a few classmates, we'd been cramming for an exam about waves and optics and contemplating why our accomplished physics teacher taught at our poorly ranked public high school. Cost of living? Witness protection? He actually likes Sandusky? When we left, our classmates were writing formulas on their wrists with fine-point markers.

Let's drive until we hit civilisation, I said.

You stared straight ahead at something, it seemed, that couldn't be seen.

Somewhere with a bookstore, I said, like a real bookstore. One with a poetry section that's more than one shelf.

You squeezed the steering wheel and suddenly your pale knuckles looked cartoonish, like a badly rendered, unshaded drawing of knuckles. I barely glanced at your face. I sensed you were resisting tears.

You told me I was important to you. I told you I knew that, and you said, No, really, you're the only one who understands me.

You turned, looked at me, then quickly looked away. I had never seen you cry before. I hadn't seen many teenage boys cry, but I didn't say that.

I know you understand this, you said. I just get so lonely.

This is probably my favourite memory of us.

I know youre sad now, I said, but I promise this will be a happy memory someday. Us at this perfectly straight stop sign.

You nodded, and I wonder if I explained my observation, or if my observation was insightful enough to imply its metaphoric meaning, as in: let's notice when things are right.

The memory stops there. If you were critiquing this, you might say, Come on, Jeannie, it's a little too perfect, don't you think? The memory stopping at a stop sign.

PART ONE:
THE IDEA

THERE ARE GAPS

I already predict failure.

I'm afraid he'll say no, or even worse: ignore me. But why wouldn't he agree to speak with me? He owes me that much.

I could disguise his identity, change his name.

Combing a naming dictionary for some rough translation of *friend*, I first land on Aldwin: old friend. I picture a knight, an eleventh-century Norman invader, a sorcerer in a fantasy novel, a president of a Martha's Vineyard men's club, a child of artfully tattooed parents. Between 1880 and 2016, the Social Security Administration recorded only 129 babies named Aldwin. My former friend's pseudonym should be common, modern, unassuming. I want readers to know someone with the same name.

Phil means friend. But he's not the Phil type. Phil orders everybody drinks. Phil shakes your hand, says, Call me Phil. Phil's too casual, too laid back. My former friend may have slacked from one day into the next, but he wavered between anxious and depressed.

Philip, then? Philip contains friend. Friend of horses. But I doubt he ever touched a horse. He preferred the indoors, rarely straying from couch, desk, and bed. His white skin burned easily.

Forget name origins. What about the origins of words that are also names? Like *nick*. Some of *nick*'s obsolete meanings: reckoning, or account; slang for the vagina.

But I dated a Nick. In college, briefly, between boyfriends. I'd prefer that memories of Nick (him telling me, I could tell you weren't very cultured when I met you, and How have you not heard of Broken Social Scene? and I don't understand why you won't sleep with me if you like me) not influence this project. Though I like the sound of *nick*. So, I want a monosyllabic word that works as a name and contains a *k*.

Mark, maybe? Its main definition: a boundary. And that's what this is about: boundaries.

Perfect.

Mark, then.

Why should I protect Mark?

I enter his work address in Google Street View. Instead of his pale yellow office building on an industrial one-way street, I aim my view at the clouds and telephone wires. The wires don't line up precisely. There are gaps of just sky.

Gaps between communication...

I should stop searching for metaphors.

Mark and I stopped speaking to one another in college. He was in Ohio, studying engineering. I was in Illinois, majoring in journalism.

He dropped out shortly after we last spoke, which is not to say I'm the reason, or that what happened between us is the reason.

But I hope it's the reason, or rather: what he did to me—during winter break of our sophomore year—is, I hope, the reason.

I can't forget: I was passed out.

Mark now manages a camera shop. I recently found an online forum where he answers questions about cameras. Someone asked if a blur in a photo can be good, and Mark replied: If the intent is to give an abstract rendering for some artistic reason, then it's acceptable; when no such intent exists, it's merely bad technique that has caused something that should be sharp to blur.

If he could photograph that night, would he blur it? Where would he blur it?

My memory is blurry. There are gaps.

But I know what he did, and he does too. The next day, or maybe a few days later, he apologised, I should not have done that to you. I am so sorry. It was not OK. Can you ever forgive me?

I said I could. I said I would. I told him to read J. D. Salinger's *Franny and Zooey*, my favourite novel back then. I cringe at the memory.

He read it and told me it reminded him of us.

But no one in the book carries his drunk friend into a basement, takes off her clothes while she's passed out, fingers her, masturbates over her while she cries, and tells her it's just a dream.

I'm so glad you liked the book is what I said.

A year later, Mark dropped out of college.

He moved back home, tried therapy, became a mechanic— at least, this is what his dad told my mom. By then, our friendship had ended, though I doubt his parents and siblings knew why. Friends grow apart is probably what they thought. As with many things after my dad died, I never told my mom.

Mark, according to LinkedIn, returned to college, earned a bachelor's in interdisciplinary studies, and, several years later, a master's in civil engineering.

When we were friends, I told him, Someday you'll become a famous engineer. You'll discover a formula so complicated that high school students will write it on their wrists before exams.

Every time I think about him, I feel pissed off and sad. I understand now why nostalgia, for hundreds of years, was considered a chronic mental illness.

I want to hate him, but I can't.

IF HE SAYS NO

First, do I call or email?

If I call, do I call from a disguised number?

It's too easy to ignore an email.

Do I tell him immediately why I'm calling? Or do I warm him up with small talk pleasantries? So, uh, how have you been? What's new?

I'm not flying to where he now lives.

But it is harder to say no in person.

I know where he works. A nine-minute drive from the airport. Only thirty-four minutes if I walk. And suddenly, I'm wondering, *Would it be safe to walk?* I consider arrival times.

Let's say I confront Mark in person.

Let's say I tell him, This is the only way I'll forgive you.

I unforgave him. I forgot to update him.

My word processor says *unforgave* isn't a word, suggests I make it *unforgiven*.

If he says no, I'll do it anyway.

Why not *unforgave*, or *unforgive*?

Why do I need his permission, anyway? I never gave mine.

What would the book be without him?

Who would I be had I never known him?

I want to include him—because without him, the book will be yet another story about yet another sexual assault.

Why do I assume yet another story about yet another sexual assault can't be told? Or can't be interesting?

I ask my editor what she thinks.

Either way, I want to work with you again, she says. But you might be right, unfortunately. The book will certainly stand out if you include him, but even without him I still want to do it. It will just be a different book.

I hate that I feel dependent on him.

I need a script. No drifting off into accommodating his feelings.

If he says no, here's what I'll tell him: you are supposed to say that you're sorry, that you will do this for me. That's how this works.

Though that wouldn't be a genuine apology. And he already apologised. And anyway, I don't want another apology.

I want his consent.

IF HE SAYS YES

If he says yes, I won't thank him.
I won't tell him that everything is OK between us.
I won't comfort him.
I am assuming he'll need comforting.
Politeness isn't needed.
You ruined everything, I'll tell him. You realise that, right?
I can say everything.

I'll ask him:
Do you still think about what happened?
Is it the reason you dropped out of college?
Did you ever tell anyone? A therapist, maybe?
How did you feel the next morning? The next month? The next year? Today?
Do you remember how I felt, or seemed to feel?
Did you ever miss me?
Has my contacting you upset you?
Have you dated anyone?
Have you done to anyone else what you did to me?
Do you know what your brother told me earlier that night? He told me that I wasn't as pretty as you and the other guys made me out to be. You want to know the fucked-up thing I thought after you did what you did? *At least I'm pretty enough to assault.*
What did you think of yourself back then?
What did you think of me?

Are you still in touch with friends from high school?
Why would you ruin what we had?
What are your favourite memories of us?

Is it messed up that I sort of want to see you? For so long, I believed that seeing you would break some rule: boy sexually assaults girl. Girl stops speaking to boy.

Remember how we railed against boy-meets-girl movies? We could be so pretentious. We rolled our eyes at rom-coms.

I'll tell him:
    I still have nightmares about you.

I COULD DO THIS FOR ETERNITY

I remember the day we met. We were thirteen. I was at his house because I was friends with his sister. The three of us were in their family room. He played a video game while she and I studied. She left the room for some unmemorable reason (a pencil? the bathroom? a phone call?), and I sat there, unsure of what to say. So I said the first thing that came to mind, I just love watching guys play video games. I could sit here and do this for eternity.

Ha, ha, he said. Do you want to play?

By the time his sister returned, I was on the floor, shooting villains with her brother.

After that day, if I called their house and Mark answered, we'd talk for a few minutes before he handed the phone to his sister. Sometimes I'd forget I had called for her.

Their younger brother was in junior high. When I called and he answered, he'd ask, Which one do you want?

Throughout high school, I probably spent at least three evenings every week at their house. His sister and I studied, and occasionally Mark paused his fight against an alien race to examine our science and math homework. He'd join me on their bulky beige couch, patiently answer my questions about thermodynamics or whatever else confused me, and I'd wonder how kissing him would feel. I liked how his chin patch and moustache formed a circle. And he smelled nice—kind of citrusy and woodsy.

What's your cologne? I once asked him, and he said, I don't wear cologne.

He obviously cared but pretended not to care, and I figured he extended that same bravado to school. I told his parents, I think Mark secretly enjoys school, and his dad laughed. His mom said, You're sweet for thinking so.

But after Mark told me, I wish I could play video games all day, my crush on him evaporated.

Mark often fell asleep in class. We all laughed whenever our physics teacher woke him (Mark? ... Mark? ... Mark!) and asked him a question that none of us could answer, and Mark would look around, lost. Then he'd scan the blackboard, deliver the right answer, and return his head to his desk. He earned As no problem. I'd earn a C in physics after studying for days on caffeine pills. I remember transcribing formulas all night because if I transcribed them enough times, I thought, their inner workings would reveal themselves.

I didn't feel jealousy so much as dumbfounded admiration.

Already, I feel the need to stop. If I botch some detail (Was it a blackboard or a whiteboard? Did our physics teacher use a projector?), I risk discrediting myself—and then nothing I say will be believed. If I construct memories through narrative, I risk making too many mistakes. I might unintentionally invent details in order to build a well-drawn scene, and then another, and another, accumulating scenes until they fit a clear plot structure. But I also don't want this to be an impressionistic series of images or abstract meditations on feelings. I want this to be artful, but the artistry can't interfere with the honesty. I'm not sure how to do this, but I know I want to do this.

Let's just assume it was a blackboard.

In high school, I never feigned effortless intelligence. My friends and teachers knew how hard I studied. Some messages in my junior yearbook:

The bonfire study group was great!

Still can't believe the eight-hour (!!!) study group you organised for AP History.

I know you are going to succeed in your life because you work so much and so hard that you don't have the choice: even if you wanted to fail, you wouldn't! Hope you will get a chance to sleep next year!

In that same yearbook, the candid photo spread shows students at a record store, students playing video games, students in stadium bleachers, students hugging.

But in my photo, I'm at a whiteboard in somebody's living room (a whiteboard that I brought from home), staring at equations with two classmates.

A line that can sound cruel or complimentary: she tries really hard.

I remember eating lunch with Mark and a few friends (well, they ate lunch while I agonised over physics formulas) when a physics classmate stopped by our table, tapped my shoulder, and smirked.

I studied for an hour and got an A on the last test, he told me. You studied for days and got a B.

I returned my gaze to my textbook. Formulas about fluids, forces, moments of inertia, all of which I'd highlighted in yellow, blue, orange, and pink. I now forget my colour-coding system, but I remember keeping my highlights organised. The problem was, I'd highlight any backstory—even though I doubted the material would appear on tests. My textbook pages looked as if children had coloured on them. How could anyone determine what to study? Wasn't it all relevant? Newton, for example, divided white light into the seven colours of the spectrum— but not because he could see seven hues. He wanted the colour classification of light to correspond with the seven notes of the musical scale. Any other way, he determined, would break the Pythagorean principle of harmony. I remember looking around the room, after our physics teacher shared that story, as if he'd just recited an entire Shakespearean play by memory. I thought, *That is the most beautiful thing I've ever heard.* Why did nobody else look surprised?

But in the cafeteria, my gaze remained locked on my physics book. If I glanced at this classmate or opened my mouth, I'd cry. I knew that. I suspect he did too.

Mark told him, Didn't Jeannie beat you in a writing contest? She got first place, isn't that right?

I'll write the memories as they come.

Mark's glasses were rectangles with thin black frames. When someone said something particularly stupid, he took them off, pinched his nose, and sighed.

Underneath his regular rotation of loose, untucked T-shirts, he wore a thick plastic brace that wrapped around his torso. Scoliosis curved his spine like an S. Looking at him, you'd never know. Once, a friend punched Mark's chest before history class started, and our teacher winced, shouting, Don't! Mark lifted his shirt, revealing the hard black shell, and invited our teacher to punch him. And because this teacher was one of the fun young teachers, he did.

Even though Mark was as tall as our star basketball players, he lacked their confidence with girls. The scoliosis, I suspect, contributed. It also probably encouraged his sensitivity. Unlike the other guys, he never cracked crude sexist jokes, never used a numbered rating system or surmised bra sizes. Given the general behaviour of high school boys, my standards for decency or maturity may have been low. Take one of the starting soccer players, for example. He chased me with a hose in a friend's backyard, drenching my white T-shirt, and high-fived his friends. Behind his girlfriend's back, he'd complain about her flat chest but add, At least she's skinny.

Or take the guy seated behind me in French. He bragged about organising his porn by country. Half joking, I asked him, Why not apply your geography skills to Model UN?

You're such a nerd, he said.

Or take the school stoner. He filmed me and a few other girls modelling in my friend Sheanneen's fashion show. Sheanneen designed and made the clothes herself. Because of a skirt's thin material, I'd taken her suggestion and worn a thong. I later learned that the school stoner had aimed the camera up my skirt. He and one of his friends made copies of the tape and distributed them. I didn't know how many copies.

Mark said, People are the worst.

I don't understand, I told him. They have access to porn. This was just me, and I was wearing underwear.

Mark explained, There's something about it being someone you know.

I remind myself, *Focus on the good*. I want readers to like Mark, to see why I trusted Mark, to think, *Of course Jeannie wouldn't have expected him to assault her*. That way, his betrayal will seem as unthinkable and unexplainable as it seemed to me then— because, while I know it's not my fault, some part of me still blames myself for trusting him.

But if Mark comes across as too nice, I could come across as too defensive of him, delusional even. Yet Mark was nice, and that's why his voice belongs here. I want readers to meet one of these guys, to think, *I'm probably friends with one of these guys without realising it*. Also, I don't want readers to focus so much on me that they think about what I could have done differently to prevent or stop the assault. I want readers to hear Mark say, I knew what I was doing was abhorrent. And Mark better. He better feel so terrible that he admits, I preyed on your vulnerability. Otherwise, this project, founded on my belief that Mark was my friend, falls apart.

Mark and I talked about our feelings, and he actually would follow up the next time we hung out. What other guy his age did that?

Mark and I often sat with our friends Daniel, Garrett, and Carlos at lunch, quoting lines from *Office Space* and *The Simpsons*.

I said, Someone say something that isn't a quote.

We all looked at one another. No one knew what to say.

Garrett: Marge, we need some more vanilla, chocolate, and strawberry ice cream.

We could all picture Homer Simpson staring into a box of Neapolitan ice cream—with only the chocolate missing.

We are so unoriginal, you guys, I said.

So we just laughed at our unoriginality.

Daniel, Garrett, and Carlos are not their real names. To protect Mark's identity, I'll change some names and mention when I do it. I don't know how else to simultaneously protect Mark and tell the truth. That I care about protecting him at all, it bothers me.

Daniel invited Mark, Garrett, Carlos, and me to a LAN party at his house.

A what? my dad asked.

Local area network party, I explained. We hook up our computers on the same network and play computer games.

He nodded, an indication of approval.

The IAN party is all night, I said and named off all the boys who'd be there.

OK, he said.

Daniel's parents will be there, I added.

It's fine, he said. Have fun.

Before I left, I asked my mom: Dad is letting me stay out all night with boys?

You are bringing your computer, she said.

In grade school, my dad didn't let me sleep over at a girl's house unless he knew and trusted her parents. He had never met Daniel's parents. He had never even met Daniel.

And so, before my dad could change his mind, I hurriedly packed my computer tower and clunky Trinitron monitor into my LeBaron's trunk and drove to Mark's house, to pick him up. Mark placed his desktop computer, wrapped in a towel, next to mine in the trunk.

Your tower is impressive, he said.

I had cut an abstract shape in its side (adding black rubber liner, the sort used for car windows, to hide my uneven cuts), mounted interior neon lights, inserted a Plexiglas window, and installed a small fan. I also had painted the tower bright blue with a white racing stripe. And I could take it all apart and reassemble its insides, identify where the CPU connected to the main memory. At the IAN party, this impressed the guys.

You think I'd buy an already modded tower? I asked.

I tried not to smile when they said, You're not like the other girls.

I described these IAN parties in a college admissions essay. I clarified that one would put quotes around *party* the same way one might allege a strip club was for *gentlemen*. I went to the IAN parties, I explained in the essay, not because I enjoyed playing *Quake* and *Counter-Strike* but because we discussed politics and religion. I could criticise our country's involvement in proxy wars, and the guys would listen. I remember we complained a lot about our conservative government teacher. The day after 9/11, he told our class, We should bomb the snot out of Afghanistan and France and anyone else that gets in our way.

But here's what I didn't mention in my admissions essay: at one IAN party, Daniel repeated some rumour that our government teacher's daughter went to orgies, and I asked, Even if that's true, why does it matter?

He said it proved our teacher, who claimed liberals lacked family values, was a hypocrite.

Not really, I replied. It just proves that she's her own person.

From kindergarten through junior high, I attended a school where Jesus was on a cross, dying in every classroom. Before raising my hand, I regularly questioned whether I should—all because of one classroom banner that read: *The meek shall inherit the Earth.*

Until I transferred to public school in the ninth grade, almost everybody I knew believed in God. I liked that Mark was a good person who didn't believe in God. Atheism seemed glamorous.

You're not one of these hypocrites hankering for eternity, I told him.

I like that, he said.

You don't think the alliteration is too purple? Or maybe it's a bluish purple?

You overthink everything.

Which is probably, I said, why we're friends.

I remember eating leftover Halloween candy with Mark and complaining about a hell house that two classmates had just duped me into visiting.

You went to a hell house? Mark asked.

I thought I was going to a regular haunted house. Chainsaws and zombies, you know? I didn't know it'd be a Christian thing. It was in a forest.

He laughed, and I described the teenage boys dressed as doctors staging abortions gone wrong. I described the teenage girls in a busted-up car with ketchup smeared all over them and beer bottles on their laps. I described the hot guy dressed as Jesus.

But what bugged me the most, I said, was the last scene.

At the forest's edge, near the gravel parking lot, had stood a white door connected to nothing. On the other side of the door, we'd been told, waited heaven. We were supposed to tell a church counsellor why we deserved to walk through the door and into heaven. Somebody whispered that the door was on loan from a hardware shop that belonged to a cheerleader's dad.

Why that mattered, I said to Mark, I have no idea.

When asked why I deserved to walk through the door, I struggled not to roll my eyes. I answered that I tried to be a good person. The counsellor instructed me to wait off to the side. I pushed past him and walked into heaven anyway.

But I should have asked for directions to Jesus, I told Mark. I definitely wanted to make out with Jesus.

Mark looked away. I almost teased him, Are you jealous of Jesus?

One night, Mark, a few friends, and I drove to a forest on the town outskirts where an orphanage was rumoured to have burned down.

I don't believe in ghosts, I said.

Me neither, he said.

We both jumped at the sound of twigs breaking, then laughed at ourselves.

You're really pretty, he told me that night.

I pretended not to hear.

He confided that he hated being lazy: Things have always come easy to me.

I MIGHT STOP FEELING ASHAMED

Reading about the legal considerations for memoirists, I almost laugh at the suggestion of securing consent.

I should ask *him*?

My partner, my friends, my therapist, they can suggest why Mark assaulted me. But their conjectures might diminish the urgency I feel about this project. They might transform the particulars of what happened into some stock instance of an already accepted theory in sociology or psychology or whatever. I want Mark's *why*.

Had he been sober, would he have restrained himself?

How can I expect him to be honest about that?

Or even to know the answer?

I'm thirty-three years old, an assistant professor at a university outside Baltimore. I tell my creative non-fiction students not to ask for consent from anyone mentioned in their essays.

Wait, I tell my students, until you've settled into your writing.

But let's say Mark grants consent and honestly answers all my questions. He undoubtedly will want his identity obscured. But if I blur it, I fictionalise—and so in my efforts to protect him, do I discredit myself?

This question, though—*why include him?*—interests me more than any question I could ask him—because it leads to an uncomfortable thought: *My story isn't interesting without him.*

As a feminist and an artist, I'm ashamed that his voice seems necessary. I teach college students how to explore their stories artfully. I'd never tell a student that her personal essay about sexual assault would be more interesting with the perpetrator's perspective. Until now, I hadn't considered that point of view. And every semester I read at least five student essays about rape. These students are always women, and these women often ask some variation of: what counts as sexual assault?

Sometimes they ask me if they've been raped.

Sometimes, knowing the answer, they make excuses for the man: he was drunk, he was sad, he had low confidence.

Their rapists are never strangers in the bushes or alleys. Their rapists are their friends, their boyfriends, their boyfriends' friends, their bosses, their relatives, their teachers.

Their excuses frustrate me, but I understand.

Here I am, trying to render the Mark I knew before that night.

When Mark knew me, I edited the high school newspaper, then majored in journalism on full scholarship at Northwestern, and then interned for a business reporter at the *New York Times* Chicago bureau, where I researched cube-shaped Japanese watermelons and Europe's stance on genetically altered crops. I desperately wanted to become a journalist—and whenever I doubted my abilities, Mark would remind me that I'd earned a full ride to a top journalism school.

But one month after I started college, my dad died—and I became increasingly obsessed with a deathbed promise: that someday I'd write a book for him. He was under so much morphine I doubt he even heard me. But by junior year, my promise led me to switch majors, from journalism to creative writing. I'd either write a novel for him, or I'd write him a book of poetry. Memoirs, I assumed, belonged to celebrities and politicians. But then, fifteen years after he died, I published a memoir for him, about him, about my love for him. This genre felt right. I wanted readers to know: the man you're reading about, he was real and I loved him. He was sixty-one and retired when I was born, but throughout my childhood he didn't seem old, not to me. We'd spend entire days together, swimming, riding bikes, feeding birds by the lake. Not until I became a teenager did I notice his worsening health. He was bedridden the last year of his life. Doctors said there were so many things wrong with him. His death certificate lists throat cancer. While I never expected my first book to diminish my grief, I think it did. I rarely dream about him anymore, and I'm OK with that. Maybe this book will end my nightmares about Mark.

But that's not why I'm writing this.

I'm writing this because I want to interview Mark, interrogate Mark, confirm that Mark feels terrible—because if he does feel terrible, then our friendship mattered to him. Also, I want him to call the assault significant—because if he does, I might stop feeling ashamed about the occasional flashbacks and nightmares. Sometimes I question whether my feelings are too big for the crime. I often remind myself, *He only used his fingers.* Sure, I could censor my antiquated, patriarchal logic (*sexual assault only matters if the man says it matters*), but I want to be honest here: because I doubt I'm the only woman sexually assaulted by a friend and confused about her feelings.

THE UNDERLYING QUESTION

When I tell my partner, Chris, about this project, he's sautéing fresh broccoli and garlic in a stainless steel pan and baking breaded tofu. Usually, when I fix dinner, I empty a bag of frozen vegetables, a can of beans, and a jar of salsa into our nonstick IKEA wok. Chris and I met briefly—as in, for less than five minutes on a sidewalk—at Northwestern, where he also studied creative writing, and then he graduated a month later. Having heard he was a talented poet, I searched online for his poems, found nothing, and then forgot about him. I didn't know that he'd also searched for mine. We wouldn't meet again until a few years later, when we both lived in New York. He came to a party for the magazine where I worked. Not realising he was there to see me, I introduced him to some other guests and went off to mingle. And two or three months later, Chris came to another party to see me; this time, I introduced him to one of my interns, and I left with someone else. Why didn't you just tell me? I asked Chris on our first date—as if asking somebody out is so easy. We've been together eight years now.

It's an interesting idea, he says of the project.

Does it bother you? The idea of me talking to him, I mean.

I don't like the guy obviously, but it's a good angle.

I don't think the book will work if I can't get him to talk. You think he'll agree?

Based on what you've told me about him, Chris says, I think so.

Is it bad that I sort of look forward to talking to him?

You were friends.

I remember a night on the lakefront. Mark, a few friends, and I sneaked onto someone's private patch of beach in a rich neighbourhood near the local amusement park. The stars were out. I complained about some TV commercial advertising stars. For fifty dollars, you could name a star after someone.

Buying stars is so American, I said.

Considering how much you just love capitalism, Mark said, I find it amusing that you were voted Most Likely to Show Up on a Presidential Ballot.

I came in second, I corrected him.

I then confided my disappointment, our classmates voted me Most Involved, but I placed third for Most Likely to Succeed.

You'll succeed, he said. Also, you did win Best Hair.

But I don't care about Best Hair, I lied.

Admittedly, I feel defensive and insecure about forgiving Mark. That's another reason why I'm lingering on good memories.

Though I'm trying to determine if I ever genuinely forgave him.

I email the opening pages to a close friend from grad school, I'll call her Sarah. She also studied memoir, and we sometimes swap work. Her feedback focuses on the *Let's just assume it was a blackboard* line.

That actually feels huge to me, she writes. *It's intensely resonant and important. Seems too easily won for such a major point—and one that really seems to be the underlying question of the project: who gets to tell which story by what authority and with what significance and effect?*

Sarah is right. Interviewing Mark, I risk giving him too much authority, allowing him, inviting him, to shape the narrative. But interviewing him, I also can invert the power dynamic. By attempting to answer why he assaulted me, he'll probably come across as too defensive. And maybe I want that. Maybe I want to hurt him, just a little. When I told him that I forgave him, or implied I forgave him, maybe I was attempting to feel superior. I worry that's motivating me now.

Lately I've been consulting philosophy texts, trying to figure out my motivations behind this project and the ethics of it all.

Foucault smartly argued: *The agency of domination does not reside in the one who speaks (for it is he who is constrained), but in the one who listens and says nothing.*

But Foucault stupidly suggested: *When one punishes rape one should be punishing physical violence and nothing but that.*

And why am I quoting Foucault? To prove I'm rational and intelligent? (I've never read an entire book by Foucault.) To prove I'm not some hysterical, overly emotional woman? Before getting too many pages in, I should acknowledge that I've been hospitalised (seven or so times) for psychosis. To some people, my diagnosis of bipolar disorder brands me an unreliable narrator. Multiple readers of my writing have asked me about any number of memories described: are you sure what happened happened? Are you sure you weren't hallucinating?

And that's another reason why I want Mark to confirm what happened.

But who's to say he's reliable?

We were both pretty drunk, he reminded me during his (supposed) apology, implying that I shared some of the blame, as if I should have known not to get drunk at a party attended exclusively by friends. And I did blame myself— which, I know now, was illogical, just as blaming myself for my dad's death was illogical. I used to believe that he'd have lived longer had I not left for college. But he died at eighty.

He'd had health problems for years. Still, not until I finished my first book did the blame lift.

But why should I have blamed myself for what Mark did? I was drunk—drunk for the first time—and alone with him in his basement room. Had I screamed, I doubt anyone at the party could have heard me underneath the music. Him undressing me, putting his fingers in my vagina, masturbating over me. If I'd resisted or fought back, what else would he have done? Fear can freeze us. Instead of simply *fight or flight*, some psychologists add *freeze* to the familiar term. And the FBI nixed *forcibly* from its definition of rape, understanding that sometimes a victim's best option is to stay very still.

Mark assaulted me in 2003. Back then, according to the FBI's definition of rape (*the carnal knowledge of a female, forcibly and against her will*), Mark hadn't raped me.

As of January 1, 2013, however, according to the FBI, Mark had raped me.

The new definition: *Penetration, no matter how slight, of the vagina or anus with any body part or object, or oral penetration by a sex organ of another person, without the consent of the victim.*

The definition has changed but the action remains the same.

I still feel uncomfortable calling it rape.

DIFFERENT FROM GIVING ADVICE

Chris and I are in our living room, assembling a cat tree and discussing the FBI's old definition of rape, how its antiquated language ignored the possibility that men could be raped. And because I'm reading Judith Butler's *Gender Trouble*, I say something like, The old definition proves that heteronormative thinking can hurt everybody.

Chris is also reading *Gender Trouble*. He plans to assign an excerpt to his Introduction to College Writing students. I'm reading *Gender Trouble* because I've never read it—despite throwing around the term *performance of gender* for a couple of years now.

I still need to read the updated preface, he says. Everyone says it's essential.

I love you, I tell him.

In high school, never would I have predicted that someday I'd date a man familiar with classic feminist texts and their updated prefaces. That men like Chris existed, or could exist, seemed as unlikely as the possibility that I'd become a physicist.

My dad held feminist views, and since he was born in 1922 into a Catholic Sicilian-immigrant family, this impressed me. He dropped out of high school at sixteen to work in his father's barbershop, but he read all the time—though I doubt he ever asked a librarian for *The Feminine Mystique*, *The Second Sex*, *Gender Trouble*, or heard of them, for that matter. Still, he embraced the basic principle that women deserved the same rights as men. That said, he could be old-fashioned. When I was a girl, for example, he delivered the word *ladylike* as a compliment. He practically lost his mind in church one day when I lifted my skirt to show the boys a run in my tights. I was five. After church, he gently explained: That wasn't ladylike. But I'm also remembering how he taught me to box. And his response when I picked a red pepper from our garden even though my mom had requested a tomato. At least we know she won't be somebody's housewife, he told her.

Whenever my mom recounts the story, she alleges I was twelve. I maintain I was eight.

I forget my age when this happened, but I remember wandering into the living room while my parents watched a court case on TV. A woman said that a politician had raped her, and the defence attorney said that she'd been wearing a short skirt that night.

My dad, rattled, told the TV, It doesn't matter what she was wearing.

And after a high school English teacher said to my parents, Jeannie doesn't back down from arguing with the boys, my dad praised my independence.

I considered my dad exceptional, and also: the exception. I didn't expect most guys—not even my close friends—to identify as feminists. And definitely not my high school boyfriend.

From age fourteen through nineteen, I dated a guy who gelled his hair, wore Hawaiian shirts with khakis, and defended the National Rifle Association. He believed he looked like Tom Cruise, and I would nod, say, Yep, I can see it. He was my first boyfriend, a high school senior when I was a high school freshman. He and I met in an art class. I complimented his self-portrait, and he assumed I was flirting, indirectly calling him attractive. That's when I first knew you liked me, he said on our first date. Five times he asked me out, and each time I said no. The sixth time I said, I guess. The problem was, each time I suggested we take a break (suggesting we break up seemed impossible, as that would mean I'd hurt his feelings—and I felt terrified of hurting anyone's feelings), he threatened to shoot himself. But as soon as he left for college my sophomore year of high school, I could forget I had a boyfriend—Monday through Friday, August through May. Holidays posed an obvious problem, but I could avoid him just enough to tolerate the relationship. While I'd rather delete my first boyfriend from this project, he's possibly relevant for that precise reason. Though I suppose it's too soon to determine who and what is relevant.

I usually hesitate to describe my writing projects to friends this early in the process—because what if I lose interest in the topic? Like that historical exploration of pets with disabilities that I told my agent I'd pursue (a short-lived endeavour inspired by my cats, Flannery and Bishop, who each have three legs—which probably makes me sound like a negligent pet owner, but Flannery came to me that way, and Bishop developed an extremely rare bone tumour and the vets assured me that removing the leg was the most humane option, and anyway, this isn't about them). But I'm excited to talk about this project with friends. Sarah has already been so helpful. And I'm excited to discuss it with my therapist, Adam. I've been telling him for months now, I'm scared I'll never write another book. And he's been hearing that a lot, considering we Skype every week. We met in New York more than six years ago, but now he lives in New Jersey and I'm here in Baltimore. I thought Skype would be weird, but I almost prefer it. Right above his head, the computer clock guides my narrative pacing. I approach therapy the way I approached the Catholic confessional: keep it interesting. During weeks of stability, I worry about boring Adam. And

I'm the one who usually ends therapy sessions saying, 'Well, it looks like we're out of time.'

The very fact that I'm interested in how the assault affected Mark, I tell Adam, that could upset a lot of women.

Sharing an experience, Adam says, is different from giving advice.

And sometimes, I tell him, I question whether my feelings make sense. Whether what Mark did was severe enough to warrant this much anxiety. I know I shouldn't think that way. But it was fourteen years ago.

Not to be too graphic, but would you consider it more or less severe if he had used a dildo? Adam asks.

Less severe, I answer. There's something about the fact that he put his fingers—not an object—in me.

Suddenly I realise: all along I judged the assault's severity based on Mark's body—which part he used. I never judged the severity based on my body—which part he violated. I rarely believe the *Suddenly I realise* line in stories. But it's true: until Adam's question, my vagina seemed almost irrelevant.

Three times I type *Mark raped me*, and then delete it. The term shouldn't matter, but of course it matters. The FBI revised its definition of rape because language matters.

A PEACE OFFERING OF SORTS

My first year at Northwestern, I emailed Mark about my grief for my dad and my insecurity as a first-generation college student. I described a journalism classmate who, after studying Freud at her boarding school, realised she was afflicted with penis envy. That seemed really sophisticated. Plus, Death Cab for Cutie had practiced in her basement. I'd never heard of penis envy or Death Cab for Cutie.

I feel so far behind everyone—on everything! I wrote to him—or some variation of that.

I used my undergraduate email account. After I graduated, all those emails disappeared.

I search Facebook, Instagram, Twitter but find him nowhere. Maybe, like me, he avoids social media.

His dad uses Twitter. He recently retweeted a message Mark's sister posted: *I hope my son becomes a feminist.*

I find an old email from Mark's sister. Sent to Mark, me, and some friends from high school, the email shared her new mailing address. I felt surprised to be included. Months before, a bunch of us were at a hokey chain restaurant—one of those places with rusty ice skates, bow saws, and canes mounted dangerously from the ceiling, in an effort at country charm—and she expressed anxiety about life after college graduation. She wanted to teach high school math, but the job market, she said, looked bleak. I suggested she apply for a Fulbright teaching fellowship. I told her she'd easily get one. And she could travel to another country—for free. After I left, she told our friends that I didn't think she was impressive. One of our friends then called me to relay the message, and I called Mark's sister.

I think you're incredibly impressive, I told her voicemail. I wouldn't have suggested you apply for a competitive fellowship if I didn't believe in you.

I stared at my cell phone for an almost pathologically long time, wishing she would call. I considered driving to her parents' house to apologise. But Mark might be there too. This happened a couple of years after the assault, and ever since then I'd avoided their house. I missed Mark's parents but didn't think I could visit their house without crying. And then how would I explain?

I called Mark's sister again, apologised again, asked her to please call me back, but she never did. We never spoke after that.

I decide to email him. But first I need some detail that defuses any suspicion about my motivations. I find a message he wrote in one of my high school yearbooks. In it, he asked me for forgiveness—but this was before the assault. He wanted forgiveness *for slacking off so much*. I'll say I just happened upon this message. I doubt he'll believe me, but he'll at least read the detail as a peace offering of sorts.

Hi Mark,

It's been such a long time, and I'd love to catch up. I'm not on social media, otherwise I would have friended you or followed you or whatever it is people do. Although maybe you're not on social media either.

Anyway, I recently was sorting through boxes in my attic and came across my high school yearbooks. I love the message you wrote senior year: *Jeannie, You're a really cool girl and I hope you forgive me for slacking off so much. Over the past few years, I've really liked being your friend. We've had a lot of fun, and you've always been there when I needed someone to talk to about intelligent stuff. I'll miss you a ton.*

It'd mean a lot to me if we could talk.

I include my cell number, in case he'd prefer to call.

If he's Googled me, he knows I'm a writer. If I were him, I wouldn't trust me.

I wonder if he's read my interviews about my first book. In one or two of those, sexual assault is mentioned. Would he know that I was referring to him?

A woman can be assaulted more than once.

The second time a friend sexually assaulted me, I pushed him away but he pushed back, pinned me to my cheap twin mattress. I told him, Stop.

You want this, he said.

I thought, *He must be talking to himself.*

I was twenty-five, an editor at a literary magazine in New York. New to the city, he wanted to work in publishing but couldn't find a paid position. He was one or two years younger, but he was stronger, bigger. And we were alone in my apartment. My roommate, still at the party, had asked him to take me home. The next morning, I blamed myself: I should have known not to mix vodka with my mood stabiliser and new antipsychotic.

This all seems almost too distracting to include.

A few days later, I asked him, Have you ever read *Franny and Zooey?*

Salinger wrote it, he said.

I wanted to say, I know who wrote it.

Have you read it? I asked.

No, he said. Salinger is for teenagers.

If I left our interactions at that, this friend would be easy to hate. But we still spent time with one another after he raped me. I wanted to pretend it hadn't happened. *Why lose another friend over sexual assault?* I asked myself. *We all make mistakes.* And I reminded myself that he often criticised the sexist, pretentious men we knew. He'd impersonate them, say things like, Oh, you've never read Thucydides? Huh. And then we'd laugh. He'd also tell me I was smart and deserved my editor's job. And there's even more nuance here—because, months later, this friend would save my life.

He called me after I'd swallowed all the pills in my apartment. He knew I hadn't been feeling well. Within minutes, I'd plummet from I-can-do-anything mania to I-deserve-to-die depression.

My next memory: I was in a hospital, hooked up to tubes, while he stood behind a glass window, his eyes wide and full of worry. The nurses let him see me.

You were slurring your words, he told me. I was scared.

He explained: he'd taken a cab to my apartment and banged on the door until one of my new roommates, a subletter I barely knew, answered. He then ran into my room and helped me down three flights of stairs and into a cab.

As he described all this, I told myself, *Forget the rape.*

But forgetting proved hard. Several years later, I confided in a mutual friend about the rape. She and I were in a Brooklyn park, sitting on the grass. The sun was out, and twentysomethings in rompers were hula-hooping.

It's hard for me to be around him, I explained. Sometimes I wonder what his opinion is of that night. I mean, I pushed him away. He persisted, said, You want this.

That doesn't sound like him, she said.

Yeah, I said.

And the conversation ended there. She knew that I'd been in and out of psych wards. I asked myself, *Why should she believe me? He can be a really nice guy.*

They're still friends, and I don't know how I really feel about that. If a rape victim's friends don't believe her, then why would she bother with authorities?

Mark could still be held accountable. Ohio has a twenty-five-year statute of limitations.

But I don't want to press charges. I want to press him on why he did what he did, or why he thinks he did what he did.

Kant argued that retributive harshness was a good thing—because it expresses respect for the perpetrator by holding him responsible for his act. If we hold criminals responsible and then offer ways to make reparations and re-enter society, we strengthen our commitment to human dignity.

This, then, can be Mark's community service.

When I talk to Mark, I won't mention the statute of limitations.

I search my inbox and find another email address for Mark, one that our friend Jake (not his real name) used when inviting friends to a party at his house. This was two years after the assault. Mark lived with his parents by this point. That Jake would include Mark—given Jake knew what had happened, had even offered to beat up Mark after it happened—surprised and hurt me. But I was already back on Northwestern's campus. Jake knew I couldn't attend the party. I decided he was just being nice by including me. But now I think, *How was that nice? To invite me and the guy who sexually assaulted me to the same party?* Though Jake had seen me socialising with Mark in the months after the assault. He probably figured Mark and I had resolved things.

I forward the message I already sent to Mark, to this other address, along with a note: *I just realised that I may have used the wrong email address. So I combed through old emails and found one that Jake had used for you.*

What term would Mark use, does he use, for what he did to me?

I call my friend Nina. (I'm not using her real name.) Five years ago, we met as psych ward roommates, both hospitalised for mania. Our first night together, she told me that her ex-boyfriend had raped her after discovering that she'd cheated on him with a friend.

One of the first things we talked about was your rape, I tell her. Do you remember?

Yeah, she says. It felt so recent.

When did it happen? I ask her. How soon before we met?

Three years.

Oh. I thought it had just happened.

I was really confused, she says. I thought the hospital was pressing charges for me. I had talked about it when I was being admitted.

Are you angry at your ex?

I don't know if I'm angry, or if I was angry. I don't think I was angry. I think there were negative emotions. Sadness. And grief. Definitely grief.

And now?

I don't know. Not anger. Or maybe anger. Or maybe contempt!

We both laugh.

I think it's hard to be angry, she says, because I dated my ex for a few years. Rape is different when it's a stranger who does it. Did I ever tell you that my friend, the one I cheated on my ex with, ran into my ex on the street?

He did?

Yeah, and my ex started crying. He tried to shake my friend's hand, but my friend refused. My ex asked if I was OK. He was a mess.

Does that change how you feel about what happened? I ask.

I don't know. I realise that if I were to run into him, he and I would approach the conversation from very different sides.

How so?

He'd probably try to apologise. But I wouldn't want to comfort him. I don't want him to feel better.

IT'S IN THE ZEITGEIST

Mark gets ten days. After that, I'm calling. I don't know his cell number. I suppose I could call him at work.

I'll say, I emailed, but I didn't know if I had the right address.

While I wait for Mark's reply, my attention gravitates toward any news story about sexual assault. The stories mostly concern politicians and Hollywood directors and actors. What about guys like Mark?

I tell a friend about this project.

It's in the zeitgeist, she says.

I want to say, That's not why I'm writing it.

But of course that's why I'm writing it. Ever since Trump's election, I've had nightmares about Mark.

I hadn't had nightmares about him in a few years.

Chris: That's not true. I've been with you when you've woken up crying. Years before Trump was elected. Every few months it happened. When I'd ask you what you were dreaming about, you'd say Mark.

But not all that often, I tell him.

Not as much as lately, he says.

I think of the *Access Hollywood* tape. Trump: When you're a star, they let you do it. You can do anything. Grab them by the pussy. You can do anything.

Mark texts me: *Hi Jeannie, it's Mark. I was in a bit of a self-editing loop trying to figure out what I wanted to say, and I thought maybe this would be easier. It's wonderful to hear from you again, I hope you're well.*

I want to feel angry, but I'm grateful. Angry and grateful?

I don't want my reaction to Mark to disappoint other feminists. I'm supposed to be angry.

In ancient Greece and Rome, men were considered rational beings capable of rising above their anger. Women, however, were perceived as too weak, too childish, to restrain their anger.

I text back: *It's so good to hear from you! Thank you for getting back to me. Do you have time to talk this week?*

Memories are built to fade, or maybe the brain is built to forget. But the memory of that night still belongs to me. I wonder how his memory is different.

We arrange to talk on the phone in two days.

Chris asks, What if Mark doesn't think about it anymore? What if it didn't really impact him?

If it meant nothing to him, then I meant nothing to him— and I'll lose all interest in this project.

I know how messed up this is: that my exploration of the assault matters to me only if the assault mattered to Mark. It should matter to me regardless.

I resist the word *rape*. I don't want to offend women, such as my friend Nina, whose rapes were more severe than my experience with Mark. Is that it? Partly. Resisting the word *rape*, I resist labelling him a rapist. *Rapist* interferes with my memories of him as my friend. And I want to remember us playing video games and quoting lines from *The Simpsons*. I want to hold on to those small, soft memories.

Rape forces me to confront a difficult question: what was this friendship to Mark?

IS THAT POSSIBLE?

In January of 2018, two weeks after I started writing this book, Hannah, one of my creative non-fiction students, killed herself.

Raped two years ago at her small liberal arts college, Hannah swallowed hundreds of Benadryl tablets shortly after and was hospitalised. Embarrassed that her classmates knew of her suicide attempt, she transferred to a university closer to family, which is the university where I teach. Last fall, in our non-fiction workshop, she wrote an essay about what had happened—but before submitting the first draft, she told me, I don't know about your experiences, but this essay could be triggering for victims of sexual assault.

Never before had a student warned me about difficult subject matter.

In the essay, she described how the suicide attempt had changed her relationship with Judaism: *On Yom Kippur I wished it wasn't Yom Kippur. I also wished that I didn't wish that. I wished I could be a better Jew, the kind of Jew that listened to the shofar and read from the Torah. I used to be like that.* In five pages, she spent only one sentence on the rape—and even then: the chronology remained unclear. In my office, we discussed how she could approach revision.

If you need to take a break from this, I said, you can.

I'm over it, she said of the rape. Really. It's not a big deal.

Promise me you'll tell me if it gets too hard? Not just on a craft level but on an emotional one?

Definitely, she said.

Three months later, she was dead.

I should have referred her to campus counselling. I make excuses. Last semester I taught seventy students, went on a book tour, and helped my mom move into the house in Baltimore that Chris and I had recently bought. Chris and I had driven twice to Ohio to move her: the first time to move her two cats, and the next time for her and her two dogs.

And Hannah really did seem OK.

She planned to take my course about literary magazines. She planned to apply to graduate school for creative nonfiction. She planned to meet me for coffee over winter break. She started sentences with *After graduation*.

And really: who am I to think I could have stopped her? That I mattered at all?

But then, at lunch with her mom, I discover that Hannah left me a suicide note.

She wrote letters to you and to her therapist, her mom tells me.

As if reading my mind, she adds: Not even her therapist suspected anything was wrong.

Her mom still has the letter.

I'll give it to you, she says. I just can't bring myself to go back in her room right now.

Last semester I referred two other students to campus counselling. One's boyfriend raped her.

Is that possible? she asked me.

Did you tell him you didn't want to have sex?

I told him, she said. I mean, I pushed him away. But he told me this was how things work. That we were in a relationship.

Were you scared? I asked her.

I was scared, she said.

She reported the rape to the university.

The other student's internship boss tried to rape her several times. After learning she was homeless, he insisted she stay with him.

I had nowhere else to go, she told me.

Her family refused to speak with her after they'd snooped through her diary and discovered she was gay.

I don't really have many friends, she said.

We reported the attempted rapes to campus authorities, but she decided against using her boss's name. She agreed to stay with acquaintances.

The student whose boyfriend raped her attended campus therapy sessions. But the other student stopped answering the counsellors' phone calls. She was busy studying for finals, she told them. After finals, she ignored their calls. During winter break, she called me, I can't go through with filing charges. I worked so hard at my internship. I need his letter of recommendation.

I'll write you a letter, I told her.

He has kids, she said. He's going through a divorce. He could lose custody.

That would be his fault, I said. Not yours.

I paused.

You don't have to pursue this, I said. Whatever you decide, I'll support you.

My student did not file charges, and I understood why. Her word against his. In high school, I tried to hold a teacher accountable, and I failed—no, I was failed. The detectives didn't interview me. They investigated me, searched for evidence of lying.

I remember this teacher, my high school newspaper adviser, telling me after I'd rejected another invitation to his apartment, I'll write you recommendation letters, but I can't guarantee they'll be positive.

I want to tell Hannah what I already told her, You'll write a beautiful book someday.

I WISH THIS HAD EXISTED WHEN I WAS A GIRL

This morning my mom asked me, Can you buy books on Amazon?

She rarely uses the Internet. This book could come out and she'd never know. Though how embarrassed would she feel if she spotted it at the local library, which she visits every week, or—even worse—if one of her friends in Sandusky heard about the book and then called her? The thing is, I don't know how to talk about this project with my mom, even though she and I are close. Chris and I bought our house last year, and we specifically chose this one because we knew the basement could be turned into an apartment for her. It's nothing like Mark's basement room. She has a kitchen, bathroom, bedroom, living room, separate entrance. There are several windows. Mark's basement room was airless and dark. Then again, I tried not to open my eyes while he assaulted me.

The basement scene with Mark appears in my first book, and my mom read that. But I never name him. I'm not really naming him now, but she could easily figure out, based on a few details, Mark's real identity. And I don't want her to know that it was him—because what if, angry on my behalf, she calls his parents? If I tell her, yes, she guessed correctly, but that she cannot, under any circumstances, call his parents, I think she'd listen. But I'm not sure she'd listen. And if she did tell his parents? Then they'd understand why

I disappeared from their lives. But I want Mark to tell them, nobody else. If I told them about the assault, I'd probably reassure them that, other than that one night, their son was a good friend.

This then raises the question, Why expend all this energy to protect Mark from his parents' judgement? If Mark murdered somebody and I laboriously worked to protect his identity, I'd be an accessory to a crime. Because Mark sexually assaulted me, I'm in the clear, legally speaking. Which is not to say we should punish sexual assault victims for not coming forward. My distorted rationale in the days after the assault: *Because I didn't report what Mark did, does that make it consensual?* Really, that's more of a commentary on our justice system, which puts too much onus on sexual assault victims.

I call my friend Leigh-Anne, a gender studies professor at a small private college in the Midwest. I taught creative writing there for a year and rented an apartment below hers.

There are even more Trump signs here now, she says.

I keep looking for job openings for you in Baltimore, I tell her.

Baltimore would be amazing.

She tells me about the latest hate crimes on campus: racial slurs and swastikas written on the walls of dorm hallways. A blonde white girl wore blackface to a sorority party, and now some students and faculty are defending her, alleging that she didn't know she was being racist. Leigh-Anne explains their thinking: the student dressed up as a friend (also white) whose nickname is Blackie because she blacks out so much from drinking—hence the blackface and the nametag that said *Blackie*. Plus, she used glitter. And blackface isn't blackface if it involves glitter.

Oh, and someone spelled out the N-word, she says, with rocks in the nature park. So it'd be nice to move where there are more black people. Some of the racist white people in town really glare at me now. Trump has made it OK for them to be openly racist. What's new with you?

I tell her about my project, and she says she can't wait to read it.

I imagine Leigh-Anne's margin comments: *Performance of gender, performance of gender, performance of gender.* And she'd probably be right.

Remember when we watched the Republican debates with Deepa? I ask her. I forget our drinking rules.

We could have gotten alcohol poisoning, she says, and we both laugh.

Deepa also taught at the college and lived in the same apartment building as Leigh-Anne and me. The night of the first Republican debate, back in August of 2015, I asked them, Is it messed up that I'm judging these men based on whether or not I think they'd sexually assault someone?

Conversation ensued about how these men would behave around drunk women at a party.

Jeb wouldn't even be invited to the party, I said.

Poor Jeb, Deepa said and we all laughed.

None of the other men, we decided, could be trusted.

I rewatch the *Access Hollywood* tape.

Then I find a clip of Trump shouting: And now they're making *Ghostbusters* with only women! What's going on?

I remember crying during the closing credits for the *Ghostbusters* remake. Chris asked, What's wrong? And I said, I wish this had existed when I was a girl.

Chris and I are eating dinner in our living room, watching a TV series about a married couple who are Russian spies. The wife is choking a Pakistani intelligence agent in a pool. I pause it and tell Chris that I sometimes have trouble seeing the severity of what Mark did.

Chris spits out his broccoli.

I know, I say. It's messed up.

No, the broccoli is frozen, he says. Is yours OK?

Chris looks at mine, which is drenched in sriracha and almost gone.

I didn't really notice, I tell him. I heated it in the wok. Maybe I should have thawed it?

It's OK, he says. Not all of it is frozen. Sorry, you were saying—

Even though I know what Mark did was wrong, I sometimes have trouble seeing it as severe.

Think about how you would feel, Chris says, if someone did that to your mom. Or to one of your friends. Unfortunately, you tend not to care about yourself. So think: what if someone had done this to Sarah? Or Leigh-Anne?

I'd be furious.

I don't know if this is true or not, Chris says, but the Harvey Weinstein thing might have started small. These men, they're trying to see what they can get away with.

I KNOW IT'S A SHALLOW MORALITY TROPE

Mark texted two days ago. We arranged to talk on Friday.
Today is Friday.

All morning I research the behaviours of men who sexually assault women. Often, these men make what researchers call a series of seemingly irrelevant decisions—not necessarily sexual in nature—that provide the men with opportunities to commit the assault.

When I speak with Mark, he may allege that he never consciously planned the assault; however, he made a series of decisions that led to the opportunity to commit the assault.

At the party, Mark listened to me talk about how much I missed my dad. He refilled my glass more than once. Garrett told me, I think you should probably stop there. But Jake cheered me on. And I became drunk for the first time.

Someone suggested (possibly Mark) that I sleep in Mark's room in the basement. Mark and Jake carried me down there, and Mark said that he'd stay with me, make sure I was OK.

One question really bothers me: why would anyone carry a drunk person down a lot of steps instead of carrying her into a nearby room? If Mark suggested his basement room, that could mean—given what happened—that he planned the assault.

I don't want to believe that Jake knowingly collaborated.

When Mark apologised, he said he'd been drinking, then admitted that there was no excuse for what he did, then reminded me again that he'd been drinking.

In book 3 of *Nicomachean Ethics*, Aristotle argued that a man may be responsible for committing an unjust act while drunk—if the man was capable of foreseeing that he would act badly while drunk.

Another question now bothers me: why did I emphasise that this was the first time I was drunk? Is it because my drunkenness disqualifies me from being The Good Victim? Even though I know it's a shallow morality trope designed to fit flat narratives, and even though I know I can't please everybody, I still crave the approval, the absolution—because some insecure part of me wants to preempt any reader's claim that I should have done such and such (smashed his mouth, kicked his groin, bit his hand) instead of remaining very still and crying as quietly as I could—because, yes, I regret my stillness and my tears. And so what if I was drunk? So what if I'd been drunk a hundred times before?

I think of Mark and me at the perfectly straight stop sign.

I can still hear him say, I just get so lonely.

NO, I WON'T ASK HIM

Chris says I should record my conversation with Mark.
    But isn't that against the law? I ask him.
    I don't know what the law is in Maryland, he says.

It's against Maryland law.

I call Sarah, ask her what she thinks.
    Guys are good at gaslighting, she says. Do it for your own sake. Also, you're a writer. It will make taking notes so much easier.
    I don't know if I've ever asked you this, but have you ever been sexually assaulted? You're an actor, so I'm guessing—
    I haven't, she says.
    Oh.
    I've been propositioned. I've lost jobs because I've said no.

Do I assume that actors experience sexual assault at a higher-than-average rate? I must—otherwise, why did I tell Sarah: *You're an actor, so I'm guessing—*
    I can't verify my assumption. It's probably derived from the news, all the #MeToo stories surrounding celebrities.
    This is why I want to interview Mark. We need to hear stories about guys who aren't very powerful.
    But if he denies the assault, then I become just another woman with an allegation impossible to prove.

Sarah agrees with you, I tell Chris. She thinks I should record the conversation.

If he agrees to help you with this project, Chris says, then I don't see the problem with recording the call. It's not like he'd go to authorities.

Excuse me, Officer, I say. I sexually assaulted this woman, was never held accountable, and now she's taped me without my knowledge where I'm admitting to the crime.

Exactly, Chris says.

But I'm not worried about breaking the law. I don't like being dishonest.

Which is why, Chris says, recording the phone call is a good idea. You won't risk misquoting him.

Chris finds a recording app for my phone.

Mark is smart. Surely, he suspects that I'm writing about him, about what he did to me, about what it did to us.

I wonder if Mark sees a therapist. What if he kills himself after I remind him of the assault? I'd never forgive myself.

And I forgave him, or told him I forgave him, or implied I forgave him.

Maybe I never really forgave him.

I suppose that's grandiose—to think that the assault mattered so much that he'd consider suicide.

I can't stop thinking about Hannah.

Chris tells me, If you want to do this project, don't abandon it because you're worried about his feelings.

It's hard not to think about his feelings, I reply. He was my friend.

I don't care about the guy, Chris says, and so I'm only saying this because it might help you feel better about the project: maybe this will help him get some closure. Not that it's your responsibility to make him feel better.

I'll tell Mark from the beginning that I'm writing about our friendship. But I won't mention that I'm recording the conversation. I worry that if I ask for his permission to record, he'll self-censor. And anyway, if I say that I'm writing about us, then that implies I'm taking notes. Recording a conversation is simply a more time-effective and accurate way of note-taking.

I'll record the call and then later ask him if that's OK. No, I won't ask him. I'll tell him.

PART TWO:
THE PHONE CALL

FEEL HOW YOU FEEL

There's nothing original about my story, and that's the point. There have always been Marks and I doubt they'll stop existing. Although these Marks rarely apologise for their behaviour. And that's what this Mark did, just now, on the phone. He described the assault as a huge betrayal. He told me it changed the narrative he could tell about himself.

And I told him everything was OK between us.

I go downstairs to find Chris. He's on the couch. Bishop is on his lap, and he's asking her, Are you the cutest?
    He sees me and asks, How'd it go?
    I genuinely felt happy to hear Mark's voice, I say.
    How do you feel now?
    I join him and Bishop on the couch.
    A little frustrated, I tell Chris. I was so happy to hear his voice that I couldn't feel angry.
    That's OK, he says.
    But I'm supposed to be angry.
    Feel how you feel, Chris says. It's OK.

Nina calls, asks how my conversation with Mark went.
    He said yes, I tell her.
    How do you feel?
    I feel like I have a book now.

And then we laugh, because that's not a feeling.
Relieved, I add. I feel relieved.

The next morning, I have an email from Mark. It's time-stamped 12:34 AM, three hours after we hung up.

Jeannie,

First, I want to stress again how wonderful it was to talk with you again, and how relieved (if confused) I am that you don't hate me, as I've long assumed that you deservedly must.

I do worry that in talking about all this with you I'm actually just seeking my own—wholly unearned—catharsis, and I urge you to push back when (as I'm sure I will) I offer explanations designed to shield myself from responsibility. Do not for an instant let me push my actions off on to some aspect of your own behaviour, and certainly don't engage in such mental gymnastics on my behalf. These kinds of rationalisations are beneath us both.

Know, going in to this, that I am unlikely to ever be able to offer you a satisfying explanation for my actions, because I don't really understand them myself. Yes, I was drunk and lonely and horny and depressed and yes you were drunk and alone and vulnerable but these are rationalisations only. You and I surely have been all of those things before and since, yet this happened just the once.

Those reservations aside, I look forward to our next talk.

Your Friend,

Mark

I read the email aloud to Chris.

Isn't that nice? I ask Chris. I mean, he's trying.

He's trying, Chris says.

But?

I just don't like the guy, Chris says.

I almost ask Chris to please, please critique the email, but I should figure this out on my own.

Or: I could ask Sarah.

I call Sarah, read the email aloud to her, ask her if I'm being naive.

He's telling you what to do, Sarah says.

You mean the *mental gymnastics* part?

Yeah. It's patronising. Also, he's equalising your experiences. That part about *These kinds of rationalisations are beneath us both.* It's way creepy and manipulative, whether consciously or not. Also, that part about how he was *drunk and lonely and horny*, and you were *drunk and alone and vulnerable.*

And I really hate the word *horny*, I tell her.

This sentence bothers me the most: *You and I surely have been all of those things before and since, yet this happened just the once.*

I share the email with my editor, and she focuses on that line.

But this didn't just happen to you once, she says. He assumes in all the times before and after it didn't happen to you again. But it did and it does for a lot of women. Is this an assumption connected to the idea of control and who has it?

If Mark meant to add *between us*, as in: *You and I surely have been all of those things before and since, yet this happened just the once between us*, then there's still a problem. I was drunk and alone with Mark only once. During our phone conversation, I mentioned that I'd never been drunk before, and—as I recall—he said he didn't know that. I also told him about the friend who raped me in New York. So why the *surely*? Was he even listening to me? A few months after the assault, I did drink around him. We were at a dive bar three blocks from my mom's house. Jake and Garrett were with us. Long Islands cost less than five dollars. I couldn't believe the prices.

It's like a garage sale in here, I told the guys.

Garrett, our designated driver, took me to my mom's house. He and Jake helped me out of Garrett's car.

Not you, I told Mark.

Or maybe I only thought it.

Mark waited in the car while our friends helped me into the house.

By drinking near Mark, maybe I was testing him.

Maybe I was testing myself.

I told myself: *If he tries it again, I'll fight back.*

I'm surprised by how Mark ended his email: *Your Friend.*

For two days now, a flashing line on my phone's screen has indicated that the conversation is being processed. I'm afraid to close the app or touch my phone at all. What if I accidentally delete the audio file? I never took notes. Chris researches user reviews, says that journalists have complained about this very issue—but the app is generally reliable. Chris suggests giving the recording one more day. Then we can call the help line. I wish I had his patience.

Another day passes, and the line is still flashing. Hunkered down on the floor of my home office, surrounded by binders full of academic articles about rape, I decide to risk losing the file. I press play. Turns out, that's all I had to do. I hurry to my desk and start transcribing.

. . .

M E: I hope you don't mind my asking, but why did you decide to, I mean I'm so glad you decided to, reply.

HIM : I felt like if you wanted to talk to me, I owed you that much. I read, actually, your book two nights ago.

M E: Oh, you did read it.

HIM : Yeah. I—I'm so sorry.

M E: No, hey, listen. We've talked about what happened. In the interest of transparency, I'm interested in writing about what happened, about our friendship—because I did think of you as such an incredibly close friend.

HIM : We were really close there for a while.

M E: I was writing a bunch of great memories that I had of you and me together, and some of them could be completely incorrect, you know, because of how memory works. I just remember when I started becoming friends with you, I was at your house a lot studying with your sister, but when I would call and your brother would pick up, I remember it reaching a point where he would say, Which one do you want? [Mark laughs.] I genuinely want to understand what happened, and I'm wondering how you feel about that. I'd completely disguise your identity and change certain details and run it by you so that you could let me know if you feel too exposed. Would you be OK with my doing that?

HIM : Yeah. Obviously I'm a little uncomfortable.

M E: Yeah, sure. I wouldn't want to be written about.

HIM : If it's something you think you want to do, I'm not going to stop you.

I'M NOT GOING TO STOP YOU

I thought I could transcribe the call in one go, but hearing his voice is hard. Even harder: hearing my voice, registering its reassuring tone. Leigh-Anne calls, asks how the conversation went.

When I talked to Mark, I tell her, I immediately comforted him, told him how grateful I was that he agreed to talk to me. It didn't feel fake when I comforted him. I even told him that I'd run the manuscript by him—for his approval.

That's definitely a performance of gender, she says.

Are you disappointed in me? I ask her.

Jeannie, I respect what you're doing.

I claimed that I'd change some details to protect his identity, but no way am I changing details. I'm not changing anything except for names. Do names count as details?

Next time I talk to him, I'll clarify that I'll change names, leave out identifying details irrelevant to the project, and that's all. Then, he can decide whether or not to continue.

And if he decides against answering any more questions? I'd likely still use our conversation, word for word. Why should I give up on my project because of his disapproval? Unless, legally speaking, I need his approval.

I feel sick to my stomach. I drag my wastebasket closer to my chair.

I implied to Mark that things between us were OK. But if that were the case, I wouldn't be writing this book.

Had Mark never assaulted me, would we have stayed friends? Probably not. I don't talk to anyone else from high school. But I wish we'd drifted apart because of distance.

I should have told him that I recorded the call. But I will tell him. Next time. Next time I will definitely tell him. But if I tell him, what if he gets mad and withdraws his consent?

I won't feel good about any of this without his consent.

When I started this project, the working title was *If He Says No*. But my editor says the title no longer fits. I want it to fit. I really like the title. She came up with it.

I tell her, He could still say no. He could decide he doesn't want to do this anymore. I could play on the concept of consent—how it can be given and taken back at any time.

We don't have to worry about the title now, she says. I think the right one will come along.

Mark said he won't stop me, but he also doesn't want this. Does that make my project an equal and opposite reaction to the assault? *Equal and Opposite*, maybe? A play on Newton's third law?

Too boring.

I told myself, *Don't reassure him*—and then I reassured him. *Don't Reassure Him*—does that work? An imperative title implies I'm giving advice. And I don't want to give advice. Also, it's a terrible title.

Why did I reassure him? *No, hey, listen. We've talked about what happened.* I told myself I wouldn't do that. Though I doubt yelling at him would have accomplished much in the way of gathering information. Still, I'm angry at myself for reassuring him before he even agreed to this project. I'd like to claim I was manipulating him, putting him at ease so that he would agree to participate, yet I slipped so easily into comforting him because his discomfort made me so uncomfortable. We used to be friends.

But why should I get frustrated with myself for any of this? I want to feel angry at Mark.

So let me turn to some bad memories.

Here's one: earlier that night, the night he assaulted me, Mark picked me up at my mom's house. I motioned for Mark to join me in the kitchen, where my mom was scrubbing the counters. She offered Mark a soda, and he said he was OK. He said we should be going. I wanted to linger, wanted to gauge whether she'd be OK alone. She'd been crying a lot, talking about how much she missed my dad. The year prior, he died in that same house. I don't remember what in our conversation prompted her to tell me, At least I'll be with your dad someday.

Mark said, I don't believe in an afterlife.

My mom said she did—not in a combative way. But Mark repeated his position, insisted that an afterlife made no sense.

My mom went in the bathroom to cry, and I glared at him.

Why'd you have to do that? I asked him.

He shrugged.

That was a jerk thing to do.

It's what I believe, he said.

He went out to the car, where his brother was waiting. I asked my mom if she was OK. I apologised for Mark.

Go, she said. You should have fun with your friends.

In the car, I told Mark, Did you really need to say that?

I'm sick of Christians pushing their beliefs.

She's not a fucking missionary, I said to him. She's a grieving widow.

Thinking back, I can summon anger (some anger anyway) at Mark's coldness toward my mom. But why can't I break off some of that anger, share it with the assault?

The assault. I haven't described it, not in some slowed-down scene. Reconstructing it might be tough emotionally, but that's not really why I've withheld the scene. Until this moment, I felt more concerned about the reader's impressions of Mark than I did about sharing my own memories of that night. But now I feel less concerned about his likeability—because he has agreed to this project, a decision that could afford him at least moderate likeability among some readers. OK, so that means I do still think about his likeability. I could delete this rationale, or revise my stated motivations. But I would only be doing that in an effort to please or impress others. And I want to be honest here. Otherwise, why do this? This is a memoir, not a manifesto.

So, the assault. First, let me set the scene. I remember posters of women in bikinis. I remember issues of *Playboy* and *Maxim* in the living room, the kitchen, the bathroom. The house belonged to Jake's uncle, a single guy in his forties or fifties. Jake and Mark also lived there. Mark rented the basement.

Jake's uncle would be leaving for a business trip. But first, he wanted to show me around.

Look at this, he told me.

He held open a 1970s issue of *Playboy*.

Back then, he said, the women didn't wax. I like that.

I forced a smile. Was he trying to demonstrate a progressive view about women's body hair?

Then my friend Amber (not her real name) arrived.

I whispered to Amber that Jake's uncle was a creep.

Pretty soon, more friends arrived. All in all, though, fewer than twelve of us were there. I knew everyone there. I trusted everyone there. So I drank.

Before I passed out, I remember saying, My dad is dead, but my newspaper adviser is still alive.

I remember being carried down steep steps—from the living room to Mark's basement room. Jake and Mark put me in Mark's bed.

I remember Mark telling Jake, I'll wait down here with her. Make sure she's OK.

Jake left. When the door closed, the music upstairs disappeared. Alarm signals went off inside me. And yet I fell back asleep.

I woke up to Mark taking off my clothes. He instructed me to be quiet. I became rigid, like an animal who senses it's impossible to bolt.

You're dreaming, he said.

He pulled my jeans off me.

He slid my underwear to my ankles.

He pulled up my shirt to my neck.

He pushed up my bra.

He told me to be quiet.

The basement was cold. I shivered, felt numb.

I cried, quietly, as if in public.

Shh, he whispered, kneeling next to me. It's just a dream.

His fingers went inside me.

It's just a dream, he said.

I remember thinking, *He could hurt me.* I remember thinking, *He is hurting me.*

I've liked you for so long now, he said.

His fingers went so deep inside me I felt dizzy.

I felt scared.

I felt strangely afraid of embarrassing him.

He was my friend.

It's OK, he said. It's OK. Everything is going to be OK.

He sounded like he was putting a child to sleep. I told myself this was happening to someone else.

He took his fingers out of me and started masturbating over me.

I briefly opened my eyes. The way his eyes fixed on nothing, he looked blind.

After he finished, he stumbled away. I slowly sat up, looked around. He was passed out on a cot, or a couch, in the corner.

I got dressed, ran upstairs, and found Amber.

What happened? she asked and wiped away some of my tears.

Mark, I said.

I'm getting Jake, she said.

Jake came over.

What happened? he said.

Mark raped her, Amber said.

No, I said. He just took my clothes off me. He—

He what? Jake asked.

I couldn't speak.

He what? Jake repeated.

He took off my clothes, fingered me, and told me to be quiet. Said that it was just a dream. I got scared. I didn't stop him.

I'll beat the shit out of him, Jake said.

No, I said.

That's still rape, Amber said.

No, it's not, I said.

...

M E: I'm interested in writing about us, because I want to understand, I want to believe, that it's possible to be a good person, a really good person, who makes a mistake.

HIM : You know, I was thinking along similar lines, and one of the things that was hard for me after that—it changes the sort of story you can tell about yourself.

Like, I thought I was somewhat good, or one of the good guys. That wasn't a fiction that I felt I could maintain after that.

ME: I remember blaming myself. Because I had heard you dropped out of college. And I thought, Maybe I didn't forgive him properly.

HIM: No, that wasn't you. I was a mess generally. When I left college, that was a good year, year and a half, later. And I just had a breakdown. I needed to get away for a while.

ME: Do you know what it was?

HIM: I was just stressed out. I think we've talked, but I just have—especially back then—such severe anxiety and depression, and I was so isolated that it just—between that as a background, the course load at college, I just—I got to a point where I couldn't go into the buildings. And so my work suffered. And eventually I decided it wasn't worth it anymore. And dropped out for about a year. And then I went back and at that point it didn't work out for me to finish the physics degree because I needed two years of a language, and I didn't want to take two years of Spanish, and so I sort of made up an independent studies type of degree. Then I graduated in the winter of '08, just in time for the depression. So I ended up, I actually ended up working as a mechanic. I did it as something just to keep myself busy. That went on for a couple years. And then I also took a part-time job in the winter doing taxes. So yeah, I've been around. But then the shop went bust. So I ended up doing taxes, but I decided that if I was going to be doing taxes, I should go to accounting school, but I didn't want to do that. So I enrolled in a graduate engineering programme. And then I finished that and got cold feet. By the end of the master's programme I wasn't really in love with the idea of being an engineer either. But somewhere, maybe my second semester of grad school, I ran into Heather [not her real name]. And she mentioned that her brother, Sam [not his real name], had a camera rental business and needed help. So I started working for him. And now I manage the shop.

M E: I haven't talked to Heather in I don't know how long. I fell out of touch with people. Well, you read the book. After what happened between us, I remember running into Amber, and I was crying, and then Jake came over and I couldn't really explain. I told them, It wasn't as serious as you think. I never talked about it with any of our friends. Amber was the only one, sort of. And after that, Jake had invited a bunch of people to a party and included us both on the email. And I thought, OK, maybe it wasn't a huge deal.

HIM : No, it was a huge deal. It was a huge betrayal. I've felt terrible about it for however many years now. I have to admit I was pretty surprised to hear from you. I kind of assumed I never would again.

THE WHOLE BANALITY OF EVIL THING

I rewind and listen to the recording over again:

No, it was a huge deal. It was a huge betrayal.

No, it was a huge deal. It was a huge betrayal.

No, it was a huge deal. It was a huge betrayal.

This is what I wanted. So why do I not know how I feel?

I call my friend Rebekah, a novelist and journalist in Chicago. She and I met last fall. After reading my essay about how Nina and I became friends in the psych ward, Rebekah emailed me, sharing her experiences with mania. Soon we were talking on the phone. When I read at a feminist bookstore in Chicago, Rebekah came to the event—and then we spent the evening and next morning together, just talking. And we've talked almost every week since. I love that an essay about one friendship gave me another.

Rebekah says, You're wrestling with a really important question, which is, how can someone who seems so harmless or acts so well or is so intelligent be capable of committing what is understandably kind of an evil act and how can it happen? I'm going into the whole banality of evil thing— but not in an Arendtian sense, more in like a *how can that act occur in such a commonplace setting*—and now you're going back and talking to the guy and the guy is still himself. It's just fascinating to me. It's a fascinating work of journalism and memoir. I think that a lot of what gets shown online is conforming to a very flat intersectional narrative, simply because it has to be flat, it has to be blunt, or else it's not consumable. Your narrative is to be chewed and thought over and reflected upon in a way that maybe #MeToo isn't. #MeToo is more political activism. I think I would do the exact same, be the exact same way as you are, figuring this all out.

Mark said the assault changed the story he could tell about himself. It changed my personal narrative too—or it confirmed what I'd suspected but was afraid to admit: I cared too much about pleasing men. I didn't stop Mark partly because I didn't want to embarrass him. *What sort of feminist acts like that?* I asked myself—instead of asking, *What sort of friend does what Mark did?*

And now, listening to myself reassure him, I'm again asking myself, *What sort of feminist acts like that?*

I reread the scene of the assault, of Mark putting his fingers in my vagina. He pressed them as far as they would go, as if trying to make the space inside me bigger. I remember a picture from a psychology textbook. Sketched by a child sexually abused by her uncle, the picture depicted the uncle as a giant. His head reached the ceiling. But the girl looked so small she could have been an insect.

Some pressure pushes against my eyes from behind. My forehead aches. I retrieve some ibuprofen from the bathroom vanity and catch my reflection. Waterproof mascara? Either the packaging lied or my tears are made of something else. I wash my face and then return to my desk and the audio.

...

ME: Well, we had talked afterward. Remember? You met that guy I dated through most of college. It was the last time I may have seen you. It was at a wings restaurant in a strip mall. That's kind of a sad memory. [We laugh.] Anyway, my college boyfriend went. And you didn't know that he knew. I didn't tell him that you were going to be there until shortly before. He was not going to go in. And I really wanted him to meet all my friends. So I made him. Afterward, though, he said, I can't believe you made me do that. I think that was the last time I saw you.

HIM: My memory is so selective. I only hang on to the stuff I really regret.

I CAN'T BELIEVE YOU MADE ME DO THAT

Outside it was probably dark. It was winter. The living room blinds were closed. Mark had destroyed our friendship, but there I was, still at the party, watching the basement door, hoping it wouldn't open, hoping Mark would stay down there, hoping that what had happened hadn't happened, but I knew it had happened because Amber was telling me again, That's rape.

No, it's not, I told her.

Jake said, I want to beat him up.

No, I told Jake, just forget about it.

Garrett, Carlos, Mark's brother, they were all asleep. Whichever other friends were there were also asleep. Mark, was he asleep? I watched the basement door do nothing.

My LeBaron was parked in my mom's garage, more than an hour's drive away. I didn't want to ask anyone to drive me back this late.

I called my college boyfriend, told him what had happened. We'd met a few months before at rescon training at Northwestern. Rescons, or residential consultants, were students hired to offer tech support to other students. At the first training session, I raised my hand, asked if the university network supported Linux, and it was as if I'd just thrown bread at a bunch of seagulls. The guys clustered around me during the lunch break. One guy asked me what I studied, and I said journalism but that I really wanted to major in creative writing. He said that even though he majored in computer science, he loved poetry—and I asked him for his number that afternoon. He and I would date for the next three years.

When I called my college boyfriend from the party, he was with his family, in North Dakota for the holidays. I described what Mark had done.

I am so sorry, I told him. I was drinking, but I thought it'd be OK.

You shouldn't apologise, he said. That's a crime. That's rape.

It's not rape, I told him. He used his fingers.

I can fly to Ohio, he said. I want to know where that guy lives.

No, I said. I'm sorry. I shouldn't have said anything. I don't know why I called.

Report him. Right now.

But it wasn't rape.

The next morning, somebody drove me to my mom's house. I forget who (definitely not Mark). I forget what we talked about (probably not Mark). All I distinctly remember of that day: my mom was standing where our Christmas tree usually stood, but this December there was no tree—not that I cared. The year before, my dad had died.

I can't believe he's gone, she said.

I tried not to look at her, and looked, and looked away. Her eyes were wet. And I thought, *Why tell her? She might tell Mark's parents. Why ruin their Christmas?*

That same day, or maybe a few days later, Mark called and apologised.

We all make mistakes, I said. Just read Salinger's *Franny and Zooey*. Tell me what you think of it.

What was I thinking?

A week or so passed before Mark called again, said he'd read and loved *Franny and Zooey*.

Strange that I asked him to read *Franny and Zooey*, considering how much I loved it. Was I rewarding him? Shouldn't I have asked him to read long legal cases about sexual assault, or philosophical texts about morality?

You asked him to read *Franny and Zooey?* That's it? my college boyfriend asked.

I know, I said. It's a weird response. I'm sorry.

You don't have to apologise to me.

My college boyfriend was a great boyfriend. Friday nights, we'd order pizza and listen to poetry recordings in his dorm. When writers visited campus, he'd go to their readings because I'd want to go. And when I was inside depressive and manic episodes (though, at the time, I didn't know I had bipolar disorder), he patiently stayed with me. The thing with Mark, though—it bothered my college boyfriend. He seemed angry at me for forgiving, or supposedly forgiving, Mark. Maybe I'm concluding this based on a single memory—and the problem with highlighting a single memory instead of many memories of a person: suddenly that single memory stands in for that person's entire being.

I remember it was summer. I'd made plans for my college boyfriend and my friends to meet. At a wings restaurant in a strip mall. Mark heard about it, and apparently invited himself along. I didn't tell my boyfriend that Mark would be there, not until we approached the restaurant.

I'm not going, then, my boyfriend said. Not if he's going to be there.

He turned around.

Please, I said. I already told Mark I forgave him.

I can't forgive him, he said.

I want my friends to meet you.

I don't want to meet him, my boyfriend said.

I followed him back to the car.

I don't want to see Mark either, I said, but my other friends are in there. I know it's not fair to you.

My boyfriend got out of the car and slammed the door, and we went into the restaurant.

Mark shook my boyfriend's hand.

It's good to meet you, Mark said.

My boyfriend grimaced.

Afterward, back in the car, he said, I can't believe you made me do that.

That was the last time I saw Mark.

. . .

ME: Do you have a favourite memory of us? I mean, I want to write about what a great friendship we had.

HIM: In high school we had so many fun nights. It seemed like endless summers of hanging out and watching movies and talking and staying up too late. That was a lot of fun. And then I remember in college, it seemed like, it seemed like in some ways we were both really close friends and also each other's sounding boards. Because I remember it seemed like we would talk for hours. And I don't talk on the phone for five minutes.

ME: I remember that. Just a few days ago, after suggesting that we talk, I thought, If he agrees to a phone call, then he must really feel bad. [We laugh.] But we did talk on the phone a lot, right?

HIM: A lot of it was we were both struggling in different ways. I remember those phone calls rather fondly. I don't remember specific phone calls. It felt nice to be that close to somebody far away. I didn't have a lot of people in my life, especially at that time, and just to feel understood was really nice. I got the impression a lot, especially after your father died, that obviously you were struggling, and it felt good to try to help you through that. I don't know.

M E: I think about our friendship, though, and the type of friend, whatever friend you are—the stuff that happened with my newspaper adviser.

HIM : I think I got more details out of your book than I ever did out of you about exactly what had happened.

M E: I ended up cutting a lot from the book. But yeah, he put his hands between my legs and then later he stalked me. Another teacher confirmed to detectives that my adviser was stalking me. But ultimately there was no proof. And I just remember at that time, I was so miserable.

MEN COMPLICATE ALL OF THIS

In graduate school, I wrote about my high school newspaper adviser. In a memoir workshop, I shared a scene of him touching me between my legs. I also shared scenes of what followed: him inviting me to his apartment, yelling at me, telling me that I didn't know how to respect authority. I included another teacher in my manuscript. This other teacher had called me into his empty classroom, said he wanted my opinion on a poem.

Because I know how much you like poetry, he said, closing the door behind me.

He read the poem. The only part I remember: *my lips and your legs*. Or maybe it was: *my lips between your legs*.

What do you think? he asked.

It was terrible, but I couldn't say that.

I said, I think your wife will like it.

It's not for her, he said.

One bad teacher was believable, my workshop classmates said. Two bad teachers were distracting.

I could see their point. My story explored my grief for my dad. The teachers cluttered it.

And I hadn't told the full story in high school because, yes, two bad teachers seemed distracting. I worried that I'd be accused of merely wanting attention. So, when confiding to my principal and then to the detectives, I simplified the narrative. My newspaper adviser was the only bad teacher.

As for the bad teacher who wrote the bad erotic poem, I told myself that I'd misread his intentions.

In creative non-fiction, the author is unreliable as a result of memories being unreliable. Montaigne famously said: *What do I know?*

I know what happened.

But, according to my former adviser, I was unreliable. I hadn't been sleeping, he told the detectives. I had bloodshot eyes. He expressed concern.

Two other teachers had observed my former adviser's inappropriate behaviour. One had heard him yell at me. Another had noticed him stalking me after I quit the paper. They told the detectives. However, the yelling and the stalking would not appear in the final police report.

The detectives suggested that I may have misinterpreted his behaviour.

I thought, *They don't think I'm pretty enough to have been sexually harassed.*

I call Sarah, tell her that I'm struggling with how to include my newspaper adviser. She tells me she remembers that workshop—when classmates argued that two bad teachers were distracting.

That's another reason why the author can seem unreliable, Sarah says. Not just because memory is unreliable but because the memories themselves may seem too perfectly appropriate, too good, to be true.

Men are making this narrative complicated and unwieldy, I explain. In my first book, I didn't even mention the friend who raped me in New York.

Why don't you just say that? she says.

What?

That men complicate all of this.

WE CAN DO THIS AT MY PLACE

Here's how it started between me and my newspaper adviser.

One morning, before the Pledge of Allegiance and school announcements, I was reading *By-Line: Ernest Hemingway; Selected Articles and Dispatches of Four Decades*. My homeroom teacher came to my desk, lingered. I looked up. He smiled, asked why I was reading the book.

I said I wanted to be a journalist and a novelist, like Hemingway.

I was fifteen.

My homeroom teacher asked if I'd visit him during his free period. He could tell me more about journalism. He used to be a journalist at several newspapers and radio stations in Ohio.

I can't miss class, I said.

He'd write me a permission slip.

I really can't miss class.

After transferring from Catholic school, I felt behind in every subject, except for English. I loved poetry and fiction. I loved when authors didn't spell out what they meant.

After school, then? he asked.

I had art club and then drama club.

You must be a hard worker, he said.

The next morning, he suggested that I help him bring back the school newspaper. The last issue ran twenty-two years ago, he said. He'd work with me, advise me.

I have experience, he reminded me, as if I were interviewing him for the position.

He asked if I could meet with him over the summer months. He said, I'll make you editor-in-chief.

After I told my first boyfriend about the school newspaper, he said, The summer is our time. He now majored in architecture at a university two hours away.

I assured him that the paper wouldn't interfere.

But I wanted interference. I didn't know how to break up with him. He said he'd kill himself if I ever did, and I believed him. He kept a rifle under his bed. I hated guns, and I once asked him if he could put it somewhere else. He moved it to his closet, but then the next time I went over, the rifle was back under his bed. In college, he'd become captain of his school's rifle team. I found it absurd that I dated a gun guy. But he only ever shot inanimate targets. It's just a sport, he told me. So, I rationalised staying: he shared his literature syllabi with me; with him at college during the school year, I saw him only on some weekends; my dad liked him—and if my dad liked him, then it must mean that he was a good guy.

Hemingway, my boyfriend, my dad, my homeroom teacher. Did I have female influences?

I sometimes read Sylvia Plath.

My time with other girls mostly involved studying.

I loved my mom, but I argued with her more than I argued with anyone.

I was a teenage girl.

I remind myself of that when I think about what happened next.

It was June or July but I was at school, in the new computer lab, choosing fonts for the newspaper's name. I showed my adviser several options, asked him his opinion.

Standing behind and sort of beside me, he leaned over and squeezed my right thigh. I was wearing shorts. I remember the contrast: his pale white hand against my tan skin.

I like it, he said.

His hand moved between my thighs.

A dull pain rose from my throat. I couldn't breathe—as if his hand were holding me underwater.

I stood, embarrassed.

I forgot, I lied—so as not to embarrass him. I'm supposed to babysit this afternoon.

The hallways were empty. The student parking lot was empty. I reached my car, fumbled with the keys, fumbled with the radio, drove to static.

I drove toward home, then past home. I thought about subtext. I drove past a woman bent over in her front yard, watering a flower that was long dead.

My adviser's hand altered how I perceived myself: was I genuinely smart and capable, or did I—respectful of authority, dedicated to school, insecure about my appearance—simply seem like an easy victim?

I wanted to tell Mark, but he might tell his parents. They didn't teach at our high school, but they worked in the same public school system. His dad was a principal and his mom was a teacher.

I didn't want to tell my parents. My dad was in his mid-seventies by then. Ashamed that he now needed a cane, he almost never left our house. If he learned what my newspaper adviser had done, my dad might feel weaker than he already felt. And if I told my mom, she would tell my dad.

If I told my first boyfriend, he likely would blame me. He often accused me of flirting.

Because I smiled? I'd ask him.

Because of the way you smiled, he'd snap.

I needed the school newspaper, I thought, because I wanted to study journalism in college. I wanted to be an investigative reporter.

I wanted to investigate: were there other teachers like my adviser at my school?

Instead, I published stories about gas prices, student clubs, cheerleading tryouts, a new smoking law.

The local newspaper ran a story about the school paper. And there, on the front page, was a photo of me and my adviser. I'm sitting at the computer where he touched me. My right forearm is covering all of my right thigh. He's behind me. I remember the photographer instructing us, Get closer.

I declined my adviser's invitation to edit the paper at his apartment.

Working at school is easier, I told him.

But how do you know? he asked.

You live sort of far away.

I'll drive you, he said.

I declined the next few times he asked.

Suddenly I no longer could use the computer room, according to my adviser. From now on, I'd use the old computer in his classroom. The screen refreshed every time I clicked the mouse.

If you want to be a journalist, he said, you have to learn how to deal with challenges.

But there's an easy solution, I replied.

There is?

There is? may sound like unnecessary dialogue, but the way he said it: he sounded hopeful.

There are good computers in the computer lab, I said.

He said that I didn't know how to respect authority.

From then on, editing the paper took three times as long. I started staying at school especially late. Sometimes, while I calculated point and pica—attempting to fit several stories on a page—the sun switched off, like a light. After I shut down the computer, the hallways were too dark for me to manoeuver the lock on my locker. I complained to my adviser, said the computer was too slow.

If it's too slow for you, we can do this at my place.

I said nothing, and he returned to his desk and graded papers.

I started bringing a flashlight.

I worked alone most evenings on the newspaper, while my adviser spent more and more time with his fiancée, a new teacher in our school.

One evening, however, he stayed late, grading papers at his desk. I needed to head home, I told him. I had scholarship deadlines. He claimed there was still too much work to do on the paper. There wasn't, though.

You're a disappointment, he said.

What did I do wrong? I asked him.

You don't know how to manage people.

I explained that most students wanted to put *school newspaper* on their college applications, show up for the yearbook photo, and that was it. I named friends, such as Amber, Heather, and Mark's sister who'd offered to stay late to work on the paper, but my adviser had told them to go home.

It's as if you want me to fail, I said.

I turned off the computer, grabbed my backpack, but he blocked me from the door.

You don't understand, he said. You'll never be a journalist.

I replied, I'm done. I quit.

I asked my mom if I could spend the rest of the school year at home.

I know Dad isn't feeling well. I want to spend more time with him.

You're hiding something, she said. Something else is wrong.

I started crying.

You can't tell Dad, I said.

Tell him what?

I confided in my mom. She left the room and returned with my dad. She helped him walk into the living room.

I tried to explain, It's a teacher.

My mom said what I couldn't, He touched her.

My dad clenched his cane.

If only I were well enough, he told the floor.

My mom took me to the principal's office the next morning.

We've got a problem, she told him.

I thought of my dad, how hurt and helpless he looked, and then I thought of my adviser's fiancée, how hurt she'd likely feel. The principal closed the door. My mom sat beside me. I struggled to describe what my newspaper adviser had done.

He turned mean after that, I said. He doesn't come out and say exactly what he wants.

But my examples sounded inconsequential, to me at least.

It's all in his tone of voice and his eyes, I said.

He touched her, my mom said.

The principal said he believed me. He'd order a police investigation.

Afterward, the guidance counsellor called me to her office.

I don't think I can be here, I told her.

We'll make it so you can avoid him as much as possible, she said.

Because my former adviser was also my current homeroom teacher, my counsellor wanted to transfer me into someone else's classroom. I chose my art teacher's.

My art teacher was also my art club, drama club, and yearbook adviser. I took several classes with him. His windows were often open. The walls were always covered with student art. He was demanding, and everyone wanted to impress him. Whenever I felt sad for no clear reason, my art teacher said he understood. I confided in him about my former adviser, and he believed me.

The detectives did not.

They said I looked tired. I said I had trouble sleeping. They asked if I thought my ability to reason had been compromised by a lack of sleep.

No, I said.

The detectives asked me to repeat the violation in words. I didn't want to say *vagina* to these two men. I didn't want to draw attention to my body, to sexualise my body. One of the detectives asked me to demonstrate on my own thigh precisely how far up my adviser's hand had travelled. This would have required me to rub my hand up my thigh and then over my vagina. I started crying. They exchanged looks, and I thought, *They don't believe me, and they never will.*

At one point, the principal's wife, an English teacher, stopped me in the hallway.

Don't back down, she said. Don't let them twist what you know is true.

I'm losing sight of Mark. This project is supposed to be about my friendship with Mark and about how he ruined it.

On the phone I said: *I think about our friendship, though, and the type of friend, whatever friend you are.*

Why did I slip into the present tense?

...

M E: Some people knew that something had happened with my newspaper adviser. I would get comments from jerks.

HIM : Teenagers are super cruel.

M E: Yeah, like: shouldn't wear short skirts. And I just remember going to your house a lot, and that was the one place where I felt kind of calm.

HIM : Well, I'm glad.

M E: That's why this is interesting to me, because honestly, when I think about our friendship—and I've thought about our friendship a lot—you were one of the few people who I felt understood me back then, and that's why I was hoping you would talk to me. I think of what a great person you were, how wonderful you were, and I'm sure you still are. And it was just this one night. To completely lose an entire friendship over one night. And yes, it was a betrayal, but we had so many years of friendship. And so it means a lot to me, I can't tell you how actually helpful this is. It's not like I expect my writing projects to be cathartic.

HIM: I have to admit, I've been having a slow panic attack all week, stressing out about how this phone call was going to go.

M E: I guess you Googled me.

HIM: I had heard about the book last year. I knew you had written something. And then when I saw what it was about, I was afraid of what it said about me. And so I had to read it. And, by the way, it's an incredible book.

M E: Your compliment means a lot, because I always thought of you as a really good writer. You were kind of good at everything.

HIM: I actually had the thought reading it, I knew you were really talented, I didn't know you were that much more talented than me than I was at anything. You should be very proud.

I DIDN'T KNOW YOU WERE THAT MUCH MORE TALENTED

I call Sarah, quote Mark's compliment.

His compliment was weird, right? I ask her. He said, *I didn't know you were that much more talented than me than I was at anything.*

That's so self-absorbed, she says.

I do have an unfair advantage with this recording, I tell her. I can analyse and pick apart what he says.

I'm compelled, she says, by your conflicted relationship with power. You want it, through the narrative, but you keep disavowing it.

I'm just trying to acknowledge that there's an imbalance.

This all feels very gendered to me, she says.

Reflecting on what Sarah said, I regret praising him: *I think of what a great person you were, how wonderful you were, and I'm sure you still are.* Also: *You were kind of good at everything.* I doubt he needs praise. And I don't believe he deserves it. His participation in this project really is the least he could do.

And why did I diminish what he did? *And it was just this one night. To completely lose an entire friendship over one night. ...We had so many years of friendship.* I'm disappointed in myself, and I'm of course disappointed in him. But where's the anger?

Bishop jumps on my desk and sits next to my computer screen.

Where's the anger? I ask her.

And she nuzzles my hand, making anger—about anything or anyone—impossible. Maybe I should take a break from this project. But I know that I care too much about it to stop now.

I start to play the audio, and Bishop hears my voice say: *Thanks. The book is obviously focused on my dad. You know you have to leave some stuff out.*

She scrutinises my unmoving lips.

I ask her, What black magic is your mom practising?

. . .

M E: Thanks. The book is obviously focused on my dad. You know you have to leave some stuff out. I do feel bad. But I think your identity was disguised. Nobody would really know.

HIM : Nobody who didn't already know.

M E: Did you ever talk about it with any of our friends?

HIM : I think my sister knows something happened. Beyond that, I couldn't say.

M E: I want to write about it, but I don't want to write it in a way that would be hurtful to you. That's why I reached out. So that I could explain, so that you would understand my intentions.

HIM : It's hard for me to talk about. I've been thinking about it. I was, you know. I was isolated and frustrated and drunk and horny and I don't know. It was stupid. It's not your fault. It's just. It's just. I don't know.

M E: Well, we were what? Nineteen?

HIM : Nineteen or twenty.

M E: It was December of sophomore year of college.

HIM : So we must have been nineteen.

I DON'T UNDERSTAND THE PHYSICS OF TIME

I can't—no, I can—believe I said: *I want to write about it, but I don't want to write it in a way that would be hurtful to you.*

That's absurd. That's impossible. How could this project not be hurtful to him?

And then I dismissed the assault as serious by emphasising our ages: *Well, we were what? Nineteen?*

As if a nineteen-year-old should be treated like a nine-year-old.

This is hard, much harder than I thought it'd be. Transcribing the conversation slowly, I occupy different planes of time. I'm reliving the conversation just as I'm reliving the assault just as I'm reliving my friendship with Mark. I find it hard to exist outside of this project. I don't want to relive my memories. I want to write about them.

In my memories of Mark, he tells me, It's OK.

It's OK that I received a B on the physics quiz.

It's OK that I want to change majors.

It's OK that he's taking off my clothes.

And now a memory within a memory. In the basement, I remembered a lesson from physics: that time moves more quickly high up than below, nearer to Earth. The basement was a negligible distance from the party upstairs, and yet it felt impossibly far away.

I remember when Mark tried to explain that concept—how time can move at different speeds.

I'm so stupid, I said. I don't understand the physics of time.

And then I laughed, because it seemed like a silly thing to say. Of course the physics of time should be difficult to understand. But then I started crying from frustration—because I wanted to understand.

He closed my physics book.

This isn't important, he said.

But it's physics, I told him. It's holding our world together.

I wonder which physics concepts will be disproven years from now.

And I wonder which of my memories are wrong. I'm afraid of making mistakes, as if one slip-up will discredit my story entirely—which is why I'm asking Mark to confirm the details of the assault. This, then, gives him power. I'm asking him to explain his assault of me to me. But at least he admitted what he did. My newspaper adviser never admitted to touching me. Which is probably why I crave confirmation from Mark. And now Mark has given it.

It's not your fault, Mark said.

Is that why my anger feels hard to summon?

I need to keep going. No deleting what I've written. No starting over.

I remember taking notes and tests in high school. If the ink smudged or if I left out a word, I'd retranscribe my notes. This made timed, handwritten tests especially difficult. Instead of striking through one bad sentence or one misspelled word, I'd crumple the paper and start over.

You have to stop this, teachers and friends would tell me.

I wonder if Mark will tell me to stop.

. . .

ME: So this is how I remember the event, but correct me if you have a different memory. There was a small group of us. I know Amber came. Jake was there, obviously. Your brother went along. Earlier that night, you were driving him and me to the party. He was in the back seat. I was in the front. We stopped to get gas. You got out. And your brother told me—I know he was just in high school, but while you were out of the car he told me, You know, you're not as pretty as the guys make you out to be. And I was like, I never said I was pretty. I thought, Where is this coming from?

HIM : Jesus. [We laugh.]

ME: I know! Then you got back in the car, and you said to me, You're quiet, and he said, How much longer is it going to be, and I thought, OK, this is stressful.

HIM : Have I mentioned that people are the worst? That's my thesis.

ME: Otherwise, he was a sweet kid. He was a teenager. Whatever. That night, it was the first time I'd ever gotten drunk, and I remember thinking, It's just friends.

HIM : I didn't realise that that was the first time you'd ever been drunk.

ME: I remember I was really drunk. Garrett said, Oh, she should lie down. I don't remember who suggested putting me in your room. Maybe you suggested it. Anyway, I ended up in the basement, where your room was. I think it was you and Jake who carried me down. But I remember you saying—

HIM : Yeah.

ME: I'll stay down here with her to make sure she's OK. I think that's when—I mean, I was in and out of it. That's what I remember you saying. And I remember thinking, Oh no. And suddenly I thought something bad was going to happen. I felt so sick and dizzy. So I guess the question that's been on my mind: was it at that moment, right before carrying me downstairs, that you planned it?

HIM : It's not like I set out to do this. If I hadn't been in that basement.

IF I HADN'T BEEN IN THAT BASEMENT

So he could have controlled himself had he not carried me into the basement?

I'm tired of white, educated, middle-class guys, like Mark, not being held accountable. Does my silence make me complicit? I think it does. Or maybe I'm finding another way to blame myself.

I want to stop working on this, which is why I should keep working on this—because I don't know how I think or feel about any of it.

Had I written about the assault immediately after it happened, I might have confronted my feelings, fossilised them for later examination. Since I didn't, the best I can do is trust my present feelings—because my fallible memory taints the past.

Even though a mood ring might not be scientifically accurate, its glass stone would at least indicate an emotion that I could agree with or resist. Maybe I should get a mood ring.

...

HIM : But. I don't know. It's. My memory of that night is not great to start with. Honestly, my primary memory of that night is just I remember I lay down afterwards and I could hear you crying, and I mean, I can still hear it. And it, it just haunts me.

M E: As I remember it, you fingered me and masturbated.

HIM : That's all I remember.

M E: I don't want to do that gendered thing where I say, I don't get angry. I just get sad.

HIM : I feel like we brushed what happened under the rug. At least certainly I tried to not really confront what had happened, which is a regret of mine. And I don't know, maybe that was for the best. What could you say? I felt bad—not just about what happened—but the way that I handled it afterward.

M E: Well, I mean, it's hard to determine how one is going to handle that. But the other thing that's interesting to me, and I'm in writer mode, so, sometimes I don't confront the emotions to really traumatic stuff. But one of my close friends, this guy in New York, I got really drunk, and my roommate at the time, she sent me home from the party with this friend, and it was a clear-cut instance of rape. I pushed him away. But it didn't matter.

HIM : I'm sorry to hear that.

M E: Cutting off that friendship didn't feel, I don't know why it didn't feel, as bad. Maybe because I wasn't as close of a friend with this person. You know, if we looked at this situation using a continuum of sexual assault, what happened between you and me, it wasn't as severe. I think what made it so difficult: you were a good friend. And I guess that's why it's so complicated, and it's why I'm really interested in writing about it. But I also want to write about all the great memories. Like at Angelo's. Is that what it was called?

HIM : The little crappy pizza parlor run by the coke addict?

M E: Yeah. He would always ask me, Do you know of any girls who would like to have a car wash in my parking lot?

HIM : Of course he did.

M E: And I would say, No really, I don't know any girls like that.

HIM : Yeah, like, Do you know any girls who want to get in bikinis and wash cars in my parking lot?

HIGH SCHOOL SENTIMENTAL

Mark and I were at Angelo's, the local Greek restaurant, with our friends Jake and Garrett. My first boyfriend was there too.

While we waited for our orders, Angelo brought us a pan of frosted dough shaped like a pizza. I grabbed a piece, and my boyfriend told me that I shouldn't eat it.

It's not healthy, he said.

Jake said, Ignore him, Jeannie.

Garrett and Mark echoed Jake.

My boyfriend huffed off, and Mark told me to stay.

As tempted as I am to remove my first boyfriend, he is relevant to this project. I never pursued Mark, partly because of my first boyfriend—but also because I didn't want to jeopardise my friendship with Mark's sister. That, and my crush on Mark disappeared after I realised just how stubbornly lazy he could be. Here was somebody who took his intelligence for granted.

Mark never pursued me, partly because of my first boyfriend—but also because he lacked confidence. I now remember Mark telling me this shortly after the assault. I suspect his lack of confidence was, though I hope it wasn't, his explanation for the assault.

In my attic, I sort through old boxes marked *High school sentimental* and find photos of Mark and me. In several taken the same evening, we're in my driveway and dressed for homecoming with Amber and my first boyfriend. (Amber told Mark, We are just going as friends. Understand?) Mark's blue button-up shirt almost matches Amber's blue, chin-length bob. She wears a shiny grey dress with black branches printed on it; it looks prettier and more subtle than it sounds. Mark's right arm is around Amber, and Amber's right arm disappears behind Mark. Meanwhile, my arms are crossed, my hands cupping my elbows, while my boyfriend's right arm disappears behind me. I'm wearing a black strapless dress that reaches just past my knees. My long and wavy hair is pulled back with stray strands hanging down. I was going for that *I didn't try very hard* look to offset the dress. My boyfriend's right hand reappears on my hip. I look uncomfortable. In all three photos, I stand rigidly, arms crossed. That evening, before my boyfriend arrived, I told myself, *This is the last dance you're going to with him.* But he'd attend most of my high school dances.

When I think of my first boyfriend, I mostly think of the road rage. The first time it happened, we were maybe six months into the relationship. I would have been fourteen. He would have been eighteen. I started dating him shortly after I transferred to public school.

We've been dating for half a year now, he said.

I stood in the corner of his bedroom with my purse.

My curfew, I said.

This time a curfew, he said. Usually it's a headache.

I'm serious, I said.

He sat on his bed, underneath his tacky makeshift ceiling mirror of blank CDs.

Fine, I said. I'll call my parents. They can pick me up.

He put on his shoes and grabbed his keys, and I followed him downstairs. His sister was at a friend's house, his mother was on a date, and his father hadn't been heard from in a few years.

I don't understand you, he said, slamming his car door.

Inside the car, he complained about Catholicism, believing that was the reason I refused to sleep with him.

I just love you so much, he said, beginning to cry. I don't think you love me.

As he turned from his street, he pressed on the gas pedal.

A busy intersection was two blocks ahead.

Please slow down, I said.

He ran a stop sign.

Please, I said.

The traffic light ahead turned yellow.

He pressed the pedal harder.

I love you, I lied. I love you. Now stop.

He slowed down, drove me home. He parked in the driveway with the ignition still running and walked me to the front door, where my dad was waiting.

My boyfriend told him: told him, I'm sorry for being late, Mr Vanasco. I had car trouble.

My dad patted my boyfriend's shoulder. He said not to worry.

While they chatted, I went upstairs and distracted myself with a book. My mom appeared in my bedroom doorway.

Your father was walking the floor, she said. I told him not to worry, but then he got me worried.

Had I told her about my boyfriend's temper, she would have told my dad, and my dad probably would have yelled at my boyfriend. My dad's left vocal cord had been surgically removed because of throat cancer, making his voice scratchy and, when raised, frightening. Only once had he raised his voice to me. My mom and I had been arguing, and he interrupted, Respect your mother.

But my dad approved of my first boyfriend, and I didn't want my dad to question his own judgement.

So I apologised to my mom and left it at that.

Later I called Mark's sister. As soon as she said hello, I remember thinking: *I wish Mark had answered.*

I told her I didn't know how to break up with my boyfriend, and she suggested I simply say I didn't love him.

I hated the thought of hurting his feelings.

He's going to college soon, I said. Maybe he'll find someone there.

When I was in high school, I had a poster of *A Midsummer Night's Dream*, the full text, hanging next to my bed. One evening I reread the play's opening while my first boyfriend tried to unhook my bra. By the time he figured out the clasp, Lysander was telling Hermia: The course of true love never did run smooth. I read the line aloud to him, finding it funny—given how not smoothly things were running.

Get it? I asked him.

But he didn't laugh.

I can't believe you're choosing now to read, he said.

I don't feel like making out, I explained.

He called me cruel, said I gave him blue balls, slammed my bedroom door behind him, and squealed his tyres as he drove off. He called me when he got home, said he wanted to kill himself because I didn't love him, said I didn't understand the emotional and physical pain I was causing him.

Later I asked Mark, Is blue balls really a thing?

Don't worry about it, he said.

On the phone Mark said he regrets not confronting the assault afterward: *And I don't know, maybe that was for the best. What could you say?* And I basically replied, Don't worry about it.

But maybe there's not much the perpetrator can say. That's why jail time exists.

EASILY DIGESTIBLE BAD GUY

I needed a break from transcribing the call. So, a few days ago, I emailed some of my early manuscript pages to my friends Jung and Molly. Molly and I went to grad school together. We both studied memoir. Jung is a novelist who moved to Baltimore around the same time I did. The last Sunday of every month, the three of us meet for brunch and discuss our current writing projects. This month, it's my turn. While walking to the restaurant, I contemplate last night's nightmares. In the first, Mark masturbated next to the bed I was sleeping in. Scared, I remained still and silent. No dream dictionary required there. But then, without transition, I chased cats and dogs around our neighbour's front lawn, trying to usher them into a white tent. I've never met you, I told them, but you died years ago and you really have to stay dead. Pretend if you have to.

At brunch, while we discuss where to get a good bra fitting, I worry: Jung and Molly are mad about my sympathetic portrayal of Mark.

But then Jung tells me, I was late to work last Thursday because I was so absorbed by what you sent.

Do you think it's bad, what I'm doing?

No, it's really interesting, Molly says.

It doesn't seem like you're writing this out of revenge, Jung adds.

I'm really not, I tell them. I'm genuinely interested in the psychology of it all—like, is it possible to be a good person who commits a terrible act?

I'd hate him if I were you, Jung says. I wouldn't talk to him, if I were in your situation.

But I don't want to come across as sanctimonious, I explain. I think it's fine not to forgive.

Did you forgive him? Jung asks.

I told him I did. But I don't know if it was real forgiveness.

I like that Mark is complex, Molly says, while your first boyfriend is an easily digestible bad guy.

That's a good way of putting it, I say, and write *easily digestible bad guy*. But does that then mean I need to show my first boyfriend as a complex individual with good qualities? I have a hard time thinking of the good qualities.

I don't think so, Molly says. I think it's common for teenage girls to stay with guys they don't like.

I basically stayed with him because I figured my dad approved, I explain. I wanted my dad to die believing I'd be OK.

After they agree that my first boyfriend belongs in more of the book, I remember him photographing me naked several times—without my permission—when I was stepping out of his shower. I remember him saying, in a joking tone, that he'd share those photos with our friends if I dumped him. And—with no clear transition, like last night's nightmares—I remember that he believed in laissez-faire capitalism without considering its social consequences. And he supported gun ownership rights. Did I date a Libertarian? How am I only now realising this?

Molly asks if I lost my virginity to him.

Does oral sex count? I say. That's the furthest we ever went.

This could be my traditional Korean upbringing talking, Jung says, but no, I don't think it counts. You have to break the hymen.

104

We transition to the politics of oral sex. A guy we know wrote a series of short poems about how much he enjoys going down on women. Is this empowering to women or objectifying? It's hard to decide without reading the poems. I mention that a straight male poet I admire recently wrote an amazing poem about not enjoying blow jobs.

He feels like he should enjoy receiving them, I say.

The first time my first boyfriend insisted I go down on him, he was a college freshman and I was a high school sophomore. He stood by his bed. From where I knelt, I could see his black rifle case. I started crying, told him I wanted to stop, but he pushed my head down, kept it there.

I really don't want this to be about my first boyfriend. So let me try to get him out of the way.

The road rage continued throughout our relationship, usually in response to my not having sex with him. He'd speed past stop signs. He'd cry, say things like, Can't you see how much you're hurting me?

And somehow, I'd end up apologising.

I wonder if I ever told my friends about his road rage. I recall feeling such shame about it. I think of how women in abusive relationships are often blamed: she knew how he was, and still she stayed. But I remind myself: he had guns. He often said he'd shoot himself if I left. I didn't think he'd shoot me. Or I tried not to think about it.

Too afraid to end the relationship in person, I dumped him, finally, over the phone. It was the fall of my sophomore year at Northwestern. He'd just graduated from Ohio State and still lived in Columbus. After I dumped him, he moved to a Chicago neighbourhood, about thirty minutes from Northwestern's campus, accepted a dubious position selling something door to door—all to prove that he'd do anything to save the relationship. He wanted to talk in person. I owed him that, he said. So I grudgingly visited his new apartment.

You could live here, he said. You'll get so much more studying done. I'll drive you to classes.

No, I told him.

I asked him to drive me back to my dorm.

He turned onto a major road, and I cried as the speedometer's needle moved quickly from forty-five to eighty.

I'm ending things, he said. Everything.

I'll reconsider, I'll reconsider, I said. Let's talk at my dorm.

He slowed down. After he parked outside my dorm, I got out and told him we were done. I threatened to get a restraining order.

The next time you see me, I'll probably be in a coffin, he said.

I won't be at the funeral.

But I didn't say that. I turned around, and left.

...

M E: I have this really great memory of us. You know how we'd always have these study sessions at your house? You told me you needed to get out of the house. I remember we went in your car, and you said that you just needed to get away. I don't know who all was over. And I remember you looked like you were going to cry, and I tried not to look at your face, because I didn't think you wanted me to see you cry. I hadn't seen many teenage boys cry. I didn't think they liked to be seen crying.

HIM: It's true. We don't.

M E: And you had told me that you were lonely and depressed. I get so lonely, you said. I know you understand this. It was this really wonderful moment, and it's my favourite memory of us. I don't know if you remember it. I know we probably were in the car a lot.

HIM : I wish, I wish, I had that memory. I block so much stuff out. I was astounded at your memory in the book, among other things. Just the detail. And I'm sure you had years to work at it.

ME: But also, there's so much I don't remember. You don't remember us in the car?

HIM : Yeah, I just don't remember that specific incident. I have no trouble believing that it did happen.

ME: Do you have one favourite memory of us? Or just a nice memory of us?

HIM : Let me think. I mean, it's weird. My memory works in general terms. I remember being really good friends with you and really enjoying spending time together. I have little snippets of us at Dianna's Deli or at Steak 'n Shake or in the back room of my house.

ME: It's OK. I just was curious.

HIM : And I think part of that, the overwhelming power of memory is focused on that one incident. And so that warps it.

ME: I didn't know how much it affected you. I knew you felt bad about it.

HIM : It was really never my place to talk about, Oh, this was so hard for me, and I still don't really feel comfortable doing that, but yeah. It was, it was. Like I said, it shook my confidence in who I was, or who I thought I was. Um. I'm sorry. I don't know how to say what I'm trying to say.

ME: It's OK. I think you called me to apologise.

HIM : Yeah, I remember doing that.

ME: It was either the next day, or shortly afterwards. You said, I'm so sorry.

HIM : I remember saying something like, Can we just pretend it didn't happen? I'm not sure in retrospect that was the best way of handling that.

M E: I think you said you had drunk a lot. And I remember feeling, Well, I guess it happens. And so then, I kind of felt like, Well, that wasn't him, he was drunk. But people drink a lot and don't do that. But also, yeah, we were nineteen.

HIM : The other thing to understand there, for a period of years there, I was deeply, deeply in love with at least the idea of you. And I don't know, maybe that combined with the alcohol, just something snapped. But who knows.

M E: I never knew if you ever liked me.

HIM : And my general move was to not express that in any conceivable way that you would have detected.

THERE'S SO MUCH I DON'T REMEMBER

I started to challenge him: *People drink a lot and don't do that.* But now cue my diminishing his guilt: *But also, yeah, we were nineteen.* I also made the mistake of saying *feel* when I should have said *think*: *And I remember feeling,* Well, I guess it happens. And: *I kind of felt like,* Well, that wasn't him.

I remember feeling sad and shocked the night of the assault.

The next morning, I remember thinking, *Maybe that was him. Maybe I never really knew him.*

And then I didn't want to think about any of it, and so I stopped letting myself feel anything about it. I directed all my sadness toward grieving my dad.

On the phone, Mark offered a potential reason (excuse?) for why he assaulted me: *I was deeply, deeply in love with at least the idea of you.* He then cited his drinking: *Maybe that combined with the alcohol.* But I was pushing him to offer an explanation.

I can almost hear Sarah right now: *stop making excuses for him!*

And then, as if to flatter him, I told him, *I never knew if you ever liked me.* But I certainly suspected it, and after the assault I remember thinking, *Maybe I should have known better—*as if his crush on me justified the assault. I remember Amber teasing Mark about liking me. This was when we were all in drama club together. Amber also acted. Mark worked on the technical crew. I was given a good role in that year's play: Belinda Blair in *Noises Off.* The play centered on a small group of actors trying to put on a play. The play performed by the actors was less interesting than the actors' struggles to keep the production together. Belinda was the reliable and cheerful peacekeeper. She was also a two-faced gossip. My art teacher, also my drama adviser, originally offered me the role of Brooke Ashton, a young and inexperienced American actor, but that would have required me to wear lingerie on stage.

No way, I told him.

Later, I asked Amber and Mark if I'd made the right decision. Maybe Brooke would be more fun to play. Amber laughed.

Mark wants you to play Brooke, she said. He wants to see you in lingerie.

No he doesn't, I said.

Mark just blushed. And that's when I realised, *Oh, maybe he wants to date me.* But by then, his slacker attitude irritated me.

And now, as if to request new meaning, another memory reappears. For drama club, our physics teacher handled the lighting and sound. One evening, he came into the girls' dressing room to explain the new lighting arrangement. I had just taken off my shirt and was wearing only a bra and underwear. I gasped, crossed my hands over my chest. He glanced at me, looked away, kept talking. After he left, we all laughed.

That was weird, right? I said to Amber.

So weird, she said.

The next day, I taped a sign on the dressing room door: *ACTORS ARE CHANGING. KNOCK BEFORE ENTERING.*

So, I believed in boundaries—could even set boundaries. The problem: in the moment, I found it hard to articulate what those boundaries were—because doing so might embarrass a man. I treated men how I treated literature: I feared misinterpreting their intentions.

...

M E: You know, I really appreciate this. You could have just ignored me. So the fact that you texted me, and that you texted that you'd been in a self-editing loop, I realised, Oh, maybe he will talk to me about what happened.

HIM : I had actually been sitting in a Gmail panic, trying to think up something to say, for like a couple hours.

M E: I hope this is somewhat helpful for you to talk about.

HIM : I think that it is, actually. More than I thought it would be. I wasn't sure how angry you were with me, or I didn't know what position you were coming from.

M E: One of my concerns was that I didn't want to upset you too much. There's a weird power thing going on. I didn't want to be hurtful.

HIM : I think we both have a tendency of doing that. Multiple iterations of projecting the other person's feelings.

M E: I hope you know that I don't hate you, or anything like that. I just didn't think our friendship could survive it.

HIM : I felt the same way.

M E: So I hope it's helpful for you to know that I believe you're a good guy.

HIM : That's nice of you to say, all things considered.

M E: Well, I was worried that if you Googled me and figured out that I was a writer, you wouldn't talk to me. I mean, I wouldn't talk to me. I wouldn't trust a writer.

HIM : I have to say, I read your book in one sitting and then I couldn't sleep. I just sort of sat with my thoughts for the next eight hours. You know, it's just tough to be—my contribution to your story is mental illness.

ME: Well, you understand—

HIM: It's just tough. I'm not blaming you for that or saying that's unfair.

ME: What I mean is, what happened was, sure, hurtful, but I already was having a hard time.

HIM: I don't blame myself for you having mental illness. It's just tough to be part of it.

ME: If it helps you to know, I've already written about forty or fifty pages of fond memories of us. That wasn't hard to do, actually. I really want to write about us, about our friendship.

HIM: If you feel strongly about it, I think you should.

ME: Is it OK for us to talk? Would you be OK talking again?

HIM: Yeah, I mean, the hard part is over, or the hardest part.

ME: You have no idea how happy this makes me. I want to understand the larger question of how it's possible to be a good person who—

HIM: Does terrible things.

ME: Well, and it was one thing, and I think that's what was kind of heartbreaking for me. It was this one night. And otherwise, though, we were such good friends. You know how I would get so depressed in high school. It just meant a lot to have someone close.

HIM: We were coming from very similar places. We were both incredibly depressed. At various times.

I HOPE IT'S HELPFUL FOR YOU

I annoy myself: *I really appreciate this* and *I hope this is somewhat helpful for you to talk about* and *I didn't want to be hurtful* and *I hope you know that I don't hate you* and *I hope it's helpful for you to know that I believe you're a good guy* and *If it helps you to know* and (this is the second time I've said this) *It was this one night.* I didn't realise I did this so much.

I'm too embarrassed to share this transcript with anyone, which is why I should share it.

...

HIM : I remember being suicidal at age twelve, which is probably not healthy. I think I've had severe untreated depression most of my adult life.

M E: Did you see someone ever?

HIM : I briefly had a therapist. I think that was after I dropped out of college for a couple of months, and there were a couple of stretches when I was on various antidepressants, but mostly it's been untreated. And it's not as severe as it used to be. It's the kind of thing where—I don't want to get too dark.

M E: I can totally do dark. You know I can do dark.

HIM : Right. I mean, I never—I always assumed I would kill myself. That was my underlying assumption, that at some point I would kill myself. And as I got older, that just became what I was definitely going to do, and then if I was going to stick around, I needed to have some sort of a life. That's sort of when I thought about going back to school. So here I am. Not dead.

M E: That's good. I'm glad.

RAPE AS AN ASIDE

I reread the early drafts of Hannah's essay, and I'm embarrassed by my written comments: how the ending—which is about 2016 being the loneliest year she's ever known—feels too rushed. How the timeline—of rape, hospitalisations, and a trip to Israel—is confusing: *You're asking the reader to jump around too much.* I wrote compliments as well—because the essay is beautiful.

'Be hard on me,' she said in my office. 'I want to make this really good.'

Later that day, after an afternoon of student meetings, I brought one of her classmates to the evening graduate class I taught because the student seemed suicidal and the counselling centre was closed. I wanted her to consider the hospital, but she couldn't decide whether it was necessary.

Months prior, she'd been raped.

In my university office, on a shelf above my desk, sits a blue vintage typewriter, a gift from two former students. They shipped it to Baltimore from a FedEx in Portland, Oregon. Before I even opened the box and read the three-page letter, I started crying from gratitude. I'd visited a FedEx maybe twice in my twenties.

Both of those students had been raped.

One of them came to me the day after her rape. The rapist's fraternity brothers had watched him rape her.

I reported the rape to campus authorities, but the student didn't pursue charges. She didn't want her boyfriend to blame her.

Nearby hangs a scarf that a different student knitted for me.

She also had been raped in a fraternity house. The next morning, she left the house with bruises on her legs. She wrote about the rape in an essay.

She must have been drugged, she explained, because she didn't even have a full glass of wine.

But rape was not the main point of her essay. The rape was an aside.

Rape as an aside.

What stories do the men tell themselves? Is rape an aside for most of them?

My editor calls, and I share those questions with her.

'I feel like every time I talk about this project,' she says, 'with a girlfriend or even an acquaintance, they tell me they've been assaulted or raped. Most women know someone who has been raped—usually many someones. It makes me wonder: do most guys know a guy who has raped someone? If not, who is doing the raping? We know it's not just strangers and guys who end up in jail. It really bothers me that we're at the same parties. Many of us have the same group of friends, yet the women are the only ones walking away, knowing about the rapes that occur. How's that possible?'

I think about Jake inviting Mark and me to the same party two years after the assault. Maybe, instead of thinking that Mark and I had resolved things, Jake had simply forgotten about the assault.

Amber would forget about that night.

Years and years after Mark assaulted me, Amber called. I hadn't spoken with her in at least five years, ever since I declined her wedding invitation. She'd hired my first boyfriend as the photographer. ('I'm sorry,' I told her. 'I just can't be near him.' And she told me, 'You're being unreasonable.')

She asked if I was still in touch with anyone. I said no.

'Not even Mark?' she asked.

'Do you remember what he did to me?' I said.

'What are you talking about?'

'That night,' I told her, 'when I came to you crying. After he assaulted me.'

'When was this?' she asked.

'More than ten years ago,' I said. 'At the house he shared with Jake and Jake's uncle.'

She turned quiet.

'I'm sorry,' she said.

I wanted to ask: sorry that you forgot? Or sorry that you still can't remember?

For years, I tried to forget that night. But the more I tried to forget, the more I remembered. I can still see Mark standing above me in the dark basement, slowly undressing me. I can still hear his lie: it's just a dream.

The clichéd ending writers are told to avoid.

...

HIM : No imminent plans to kill myself here.

M E: OK, good. It's strange being a professor now. I mean, it's hard—because I know my students have so much going on, and sometimes they tell me their other professors don't understand, or they think these kids are making things up. One of my students, she recently killed herself. I was supposed to see her this past week, actually.

HE'S NOT OFF THE HOOK

I tell my therapist, Adam, that I can't stop thinking about Hannah.

'If you had held on to that idea when Hannah was still alive,' Adam says, 'that she wasn't OK or wasn't over it—though she said that she was—would it have been different?'

'It's not that it would have changed what happened,' I tell him, 'but it says something about my carelessness at the time. To not have seen my student's depression. I feel ignorant.'

'This isn't meant to sting,' Adam says, 'but it's inevitably going to sting a bit, but I just want to see if I can open your mind to a different angle. I think there are times when you reflect on—let's use your first boyfriend, how you've told me that he came from a broken home and he'd threaten to kill himself and somehow it felt like your responsibility to stay with him. I don't know, there are probably a number of examples in your life where you feel drawn to that thinking. It doesn't feel like it inside of you—even though I'm not inside of you, I know that it doesn't feel like it—but it's kind of like a grandiosity. It has more of a feeling of compassion, like a need to help. And maybe you think, *Fuck you, I'm not grandiose.* But it doesn't feel like that. The idea is that you become a linchpin to somebody else's survival.'

'That doesn't sting,' I tell him. 'I think it's accurate.'

'The grandiosity that I see in you sometimes manifests in helping others, not in helping yourself. It's an alternate universe; when you're doing things for you, it never happens.

When you feel like you need to do something for others, that's usually when the grandiosity kicks in. Yours is usually wrapped up in guilt or a sense of duty.'

What about the situation with Mark? I ask Adam. The only person who can really forgive him in this instance is me—because I'm the one he hurt. He can only get resolution from hearing from me and talking to me and feeling like he can help me. Is that grandiosity?

A little, Adam says. Because actually, it's not up to you. If he wants to get himself off the hook, he has to do that himself. For you to think that if you grant him forgiveness—and it's not lip service, let's say you have to do some earnest and deep work to try to actually forgive him—to think that if you're doing that, then he's off the hook? He's not. I can tell you that right now. He may appreciate that forgiveness, and you may feel more free. But he's not off the hook—because he's got to live with his psyche. Whatever he works on or doesn't work on, that's up to him. So you're not doing that for him.

...

M E: I didn't want this to be upsetting for you. That's why when I texted you, I said that I was very happy to hear from you. Because again, I can't say it enough, I do think you're a good person.

HIM: I'm sorry to keep not giving you a response to that, but compliments are still hard for me.

M E: I feel bad, taking up your Friday night.

HIM: I don't have plans.

M E: Do you live alone?

HIM: I live alone. I have a little studio apartment.

M E: Are you still in touch with a lot of people from high school?

HIM: Probably the only person I talk to from high school in the last three or four years is Carlos. We were close for a while. We're not as close as we used to be. He lives just two miles from me.

M E: I fell out of touch with pretty much everybody. And then I deleted Facebook.

HIM : I didn't like who I was, and so I didn't want to be in touch with anyone who knew me that way. Even more than just people grow apart in their twenties. I chose not to hang on to those friendships.

M E: Amber reached out to me some years ago. We chatted. We hadn't talked for a while, and that was on me. It's hard if you haven't talked to someone for a while. How do you explain, Well, I fell out of touch because I just got out of the psych ward?

HIM : And that's a tough one.

M E: Yeah. Though Amber was cool. She'd be understanding.

HIM : I haven't talked to her in so long.

M E: She had asked if I had talked to you in a while. I said, No, I think stuff got too awkward, and she asked why. And I said, Do you remember? And she didn't remember. That was hard. Sometimes these things that are traumatic for you, when other people don't remember, it's strange.

HIM : Yeah, I can see that.

M E: But yeah, so you haven't talked to her in a while.

HIM : No, it's been years and years. Like I said, I sort of lost touch with everybody.

M E: I worried that everybody thought—and this is probably a self-involved thing to think, because probably no one was thinking about me—but I worried that everybody thought I'd gotten snobby after I left Ohio. But really, well, you read the book. I was having such a hard time. It was easier to just avoid people.

HIM : Which I can totally understand.

M E: So yeah, I just lost touch with everybody. Well, it really means a lot. I hope it was helpful, for you to know I don't hate you.

HIM : Yeah, I mean, that's good.

M E: Really, I just felt awkward about it all. And sad.

HIM : It's a stupid way for a friendship to end. It's totally understandable but regrettable is a more accurate way to put it.

M E: Someone asked me earlier, What are you doing later today, and I said, Oh, just catching up with a friend. And that's how it came out. Not, a former friend or anything like that. Just, a friend.

HIM : A friend I used to know.

M E: Yeah, so.

HIM : It's actually really good to talk to you. I mean, it is, it is nice to catch up. I was terrified of how this conversation was going to go. And I'm glad that it's gone this way.

M E: And I'm glad that you're open to this. Not just because I'm writing about this. I mean, I was talking to my editor. I told her that this is what I want to do. And I told her that I want to protect your identity. I would run it by you, and if you want me to change things, I will.

HIM : I kind of feel like you have the right. So I don't want to limit what you're trying to do.

M E: Let me tell you, not many people would tell a writer that.

HIM : I mean, it's things that happened.

MORTIFIED ISN'T STRONG ENOUGH

Hearing myself thank Mark for talking to me about sexually assaulting me, I don't know how to describe the feeling it induces. Mortified isn't strong enough.

I laugh when transcribing him saying, *And I'm glad that it's gone this way.*

Of course he was glad the conversation went the way it did. I repeatedly told him he's such a good person. And why did I need to convince myself of this? Or him of this? Does it go back to needing to believe I was never wrong to trust him? Or do I simply want my friend back?

Or is it a bunch of reasons I'll never understand?

And why did I offer to run this manuscript by him? Maybe he'll forget I ever offered. How many times have I offered now?

Though it sounds like he won't ask: *I don't want to limit what you're trying to do.*

If he wants to read the manuscript before it's published, he'll need to ask me. I like the idea of making him ask. And then I like the idea of telling him no. But I wonder if I'd be capable of refusing to show him the manuscript. I think I'd feel too guilty because I already offered.

I reread the opening pages, the *If He Says No* and *If He Says Yes* sections. I sounded angry. Where did that anger go? Was I pretending to be angry—because angry is how I'm expected to feel?

I ask Chris, 'Have I ever expressed anger about Mark?'
     'Just pain,' Chris says. 'Hurt.'

...

ME: Honestly, really, you're a good person. I mean that. I know you're not good at compliments. So if you want to ignore awkwardly, that's fine.

HIM: Thank you.

ME: When I talked to my partner, Chris, and I said, I really hope Mark says yes. And Chris said, He probably will because he feels bad.

HIM: That Chris guy sounds smart. He might be a keeper.

ME: He is. I feel very lucky. I feel very lucky.

HIM: Well, I'm happy for you.

ME: Thanks. I can let you go.

AN ACCUSE

Last night's nightmare: I play myself in a high school play. I perform in the wings, dramatically studying for a physics exam. I turn textbook pages furiously and highlight them in angry swooping gestures. I bury my face in my hands. After the applause, I ask my art teacher, 'No one could see me, could they?' He says, 'No, but the crowd loved it.' Next, I am running through the high school. My newspaper adviser stops me, asks, 'On your way to identify me?' He smirks. I run.

I wake up sweating next to Flannery and Bishop. I am guessing they refused to give Chris enough room in bed again. Sure enough, he's in his office, asleep on his futon.

I go into my office, sit on my daybed, hold my manuscript, stand, sit at my desk. What am I doing? I visit my hometown's police department website. I request the investigation records about my newspaper adviser. I used to have them, but I threw away my copy years ago. What if I'm misremembering what I told the detectives? I need to get this right.

I spend the rest of the morning and afternoon writing.

Chris and I take my mom out for dinner. She asks how the book is going, though she does not press me on what it's about. I tell her it's going OK. I suggest we skip seeing a movie that night. Though we never planned to see a movie. It's just something to say.

The next morning, the police incident report arrives. I didn't expect it to arrive so soon. I love this typo: *so she made an accuse to leave the room.*

According to the report, my principal and guidance counsellor told detectives that I was someone who would not lie.

Amber, Heather, and Mark's sister provided typed statements that the detectives summarised:

> On a few occasions [Amber] had overheard [the newspaper adviser] asking Jeannie to come over to his house to work on the paper… When Jeannie would stay late in school working, she asked [Amber] to stay and help, but [the newspaper adviser] would tell [Amber] she could leave.

> [Heather] stated that she was present when [the newspaper adviser] had physically touched Jeannie and her. She stated that he has touched her arms, Jeannie's shoulders and knees, by rubs, pats, or "accidents." She claims that this occurred when they were working in close proximity to each other. She stated that [the newspaper adviser] would always talk about Jeannie falling short of her duties as editor, to the other students. She claims that Jeannie would have to stay at school late, working either alone or with [the newspaper adviser]. [Heather] recalls that after [the principal] ordered [the newspaper adviser] to stay away from Jeannie, she would see him following her and even attempted to try and talk with her on one occasion. It should be noted that there is nothing in [Heather]'s statement that shows any criminal wrongdoing by [the newspaper adviser].

> [Mark's sister] claims that when [the newspaper adviser] and Jeannie were in a room working alone, the door

would usually be closed. She claims that [the newspaper adviser] frequently had his hands on Jeannie's shoulders while she was working… She also claims that Jeannie would be the only one he would ever ask to stay and work late.

After reading what Amber, Heather, and Mark's sister told the detectives, I no longer seem so unreliable, or as unreliable as I felt.

But running like a refrain throughout the report: *It should be noted that there is nothing in [Jeannie/Heather/Amber/Mark's sister]'s statement that shows any criminal wrongdoing by [the newspaper adviser].*

Garrett, Jake, Carlos, Daniel, and Mark—none of them provided statements. Maybe I didn't complain to them about my newspaper adviser. Was I afraid of making them aware of what they could become?

I forgot about this: my newspaper adviser agreed to a CVSA test. CVSA: Computer Voice Stress Analyser. The detective reported that during the pretest interview, *[the newspaper adviser] noted Jeannie coming to school late…*

But I didn't actually arrive to school late. I simply didn't go to homeroom because my newspaper adviser was also my homeroom teacher.

… Jeannie's bloodshot eyes and overall physical appearance.

I was applying for college scholarships, studying for Advanced Placement exams, and worrying about my dad's health. And my newspaper adviser regularly yelled at me, so sure, I wasn't sleeping well. I probably did have bloodshot eyes. As for my *overall physical appearance*, what about it?

[The newspaper adviser] felt that he was doing what was in the best interest of Jeannie.

The following two relevant questions were asked of [the newspaper adviser]:

#4 Did you touch Jeannie's leg in a sexual manner? No.

#6 Did you rub Jeannie's leg in a sexual manner? No.

He passed the test. But if high stress is an indication of deception, then I can't imagine ever passing something like that.

If someone had seen my newspaper adviser—no, let's say filmed him—running his hand up my thigh and between my legs, would the detectives have considered his action criminal wrongdoing? I would hope so. But I'm now remembering when the detectives asked me, Is it possible that his hand slipped? And I had to grant them that. It's unlikely, but yes, it's possible. Also, I never thought it possible that a teacher would abuse me the way he did—but if I told that to the detectives, they didn't note it in their report.

My newspaper adviser still teaches high school students. He's married and has two daughters now. Does he worry about a teacher treating his daughters how he treated me? I hope so. I hope he worries about it every day.

...

HIM : Do you want to—just tell me what you want to do. We can talk.
M E: Occasionally, I'll check in with you. Maybe at some point I can visit and we can meet in person to talk.

HIM : Yeah, we can grab a coffee or something. That would be great.

ME: Yeah, I think it would be really nice.

HIM : Yeah, it's tough for me to—I'm basically working six days a week at the moment, so it can be tough for me to find time. But I'll see what I can do.

ME: Yeah, it's OK. It would be down the line. I guess I just wanted to see how open you would be to this. I really appreciate it.

HIM : I'm open to whatever you want from me.

ME: OK.

HIM : Like I said, I owe you that much. Plus, it will, honestly, be really good to see you.

ME: OK. Well, you have my number. Also, you have my email address. And if anything comes to you, a memory or something, don't hesitate to email me. Anything like that's going to be helpful to me. I can let you go.

HIM : Sounds like I should let you go.

ME: Oh no, I just don't want to keep you. Do you work tomorrow?

HIM : I do, but I'll be up for hours anyway. No matter what.

ME: Well, thank you again for reading my book. You didn't have to do that. I'm sorry that it was upsetting, that that was the part you were in.

HIM : No, but who do I have to blame but myself, right?

ME: I'm glad we're talking, though. So I can tell you: that's not how I see you.

HIM : I just want to reiterate, it was a treat to read the early sections especially. It was interesting to see how you saw your childhood. Because our relationship with our fathers is so different.

I CAN'T LISTEN TO IT ANYMORE

My dad died my freshman year, after the course withdrawal deadline at Northwestern. This meant that if I dropped my classes, I'd lose my scholarship money for that term. And so I returned to college, which was, according to my mom, what my dad had wanted.

That winter break, I visited Mark's house. Other friends were there. One of them, whose hamster had just died, said: I hate how you go to college and then everything dies.

I struggled not to glare at her.

Conversation ensued about her hamster.

But then somebody else interjected, mentioned her fish had died. And I thought, *Does no one remember that my dad died last month?*

Mark then talked about some friends who were growing pot at a cemetery.

That's messed up, I said.

It's genius, Mark said.

It's disrespectful, I fired back.

Mark took off his glasses, pinched his nose, and sighed.

It's funny, he insisted.

I got up to leave.

Where are you going? Mark's sister asked.

To the house where my mom lives, I said.

Home? she asked.

'No,' I said. 'My dad's dead. But go on. Talk about the dead hamster and the dead fish and growing pot at a cemetery. I can't listen to it anymore.'

And then Amber said, 'But Jeannie, you knew your dad was old. He was going to die eventually.'

I left without saying goodbye. I drove to my mom's house. When I arrived, she was asleep on the floor where my dad's hospice bed had been, wearing one of his shirts.

The winter break after my dad died—one year before Mark assaulted me—I secured the police reports about my high school newspaper adviser. I drove toward the cemetery and parked near its entrance, on the side of the quiet country road. I sat there in my car, reading the report and crying. Shortly after, I think, I threw them away.

The point is, after my dad died, I let myself cry only about his death. If I cried about something else, such as my sleazy adviser, then I needed to relate it to my dad. And what better way to do that than to cry at (or at least near) the cemetery? By the time Mark assaulted me, I was too focused on grief for my dad. Sexual assault became an inconvenience, something I worried therapists would latch on to—which is why I never talked about it, or if I did, I'd say things like, 'A close friend sexually assaulted me, but that's not what I'm here for.'

But now, with this book, that's what I'm here for.

. . .

M E: What is your relationship with your dad?
HIM : Well, we're on basically good terms now, but I hated my father for a decent portion of my childhood. I was not really the son to him in the ways he wanted me to be. He's kind of a jock, and he wanted, especially when he was younger, a son who could play football with him and sports, and I was this nerd who liked science, and

then I was a slacker and messy, and he's super detail-oriented and organised, and we just clashed over and over and over again.

ME: I didn't know that. I always thought your dad—he would tease you.

HIM: Everybody loved my dad. And I love my dad now. But we had a rough go of it for the first twenty, twenty-five years.

ME: I was very lucky. I remember at one point, Amber of all people said, Well, Jeannie, you knew your dad was old and was going to die eventually.

HIM: That sounds exactly like the kind of thing she would say. That's really hurtful.

ME: Yeah, I took his death hard, for all sorts of reasons. I'm glad you liked the childhood sections.

HIM: The other thing that leapt out at me, there's a section where you talk about pre-grieving somebody, which I've done. That's absolutely a thing. Coincidentally about my father.

ME: Oh, really?

HIM: Yeah. This would have been seven or eight years ago now. He had had some sort of minor health scare. I don't know if you remember this, but my dad would always joke that at his funeral he wants the thirty-minute live version of "Whipping Post" played. Which my mom did not appreciate at all because of the implication.

ME: Right.

HIM: But I remember I was living with them at the time, and I was home alone for whatever reason, I don't remember, and I put that song on, and I just cried for an hour. Which I don't do. Just like, gut-wrenching ugly crying. And it was just, I was stuck in a—I don't know how else to describe it except I was grieving for my not-dead father.

M E: Did you ever tell him?

HIM: No. Why would I ever tell him that?

M E: I don't know. I was just curious. Well, you said—

HIM: We don't have that kind of a relationship. Like, we're friends.

M E: I'm glad that somebody else then connected with that. With the pre-grieving. Yeah, it was definitely a hard book to write.

HIM: It couldn't not be.

M E: I don't go back to my book. I mean, why would I look back at it again? I feel so distanced from it. I revised it so many times. So it is meaningful to know that it produced a feeling.

HIM: It's a beautiful book.

M E: Well, I'm going to get going. I'm going to end while I just got this great compliment from you. It means a lot. And it means a lot that you're willing to talk. I'm incredibly grateful. This is helping me, actually. I'm feeling a lot better about it. Also, I just never knew if we would talk again. It would be like breaking some social contract. Boy sexually assaults girl. Girl can't talk to boy anymore.

HIM: That's the way it works. Those are the rules.

M E: And so, well, this is an excuse to talk again. And so, I'm really happy. I really am. It's good to talk to you and hear your voice, and I'm glad that you're doing a lot better.

HIM: Yeah, I actually am. I know I was painting a sort of bleak picture there, but I'm doing pretty well, all things considered.

M E: I'm a loser and I go to bed at like ten o'clock because I get up early to write.

HIM: Well, I won't keep you up late.

M E: But I am excited to talk again. And also, feel free to call or email me anytime. Are you on social media?

HIM : I have accounts, but I'm not active.

M E: I figured you're not the social media type.

HIM : I'm really not.

M E: I like what Mark Twain said about the telephone. His sentiment about the telephone is sometimes how I feel about social media. He said something like, The human voice carries entirely too far as it is.

HIM : That's a really good quote.

M E: Yeah, isn't it?

HIM : Yeah.

M E: Well, I'm excited to talk again. Thank you. Thank you. Really, it means a lot. Well, we'll talk again.

HIM : Anything I can do.

PART THREE:
THE NEXT PHONE CALL

READER, I HAD HIM ARRESTED

The two main definitions of gravity: the natural phenomenon that draws all things with mass toward one another; extreme or alarming importance.

Gravity often is described as a force, but the general theory of relativity describes it more accurately: gravity is a consequence of the curvature of space–time caused by the uneven distribution of mass.

With Mark, what happened felt less like force and more like a consequence of an uneven distribution of power. I was passed out. He was bigger and I was smaller.

Is rape not the consequence of an uneven distribution of power?

I tell Chris, I feel bad. I'm now in the position of power. I'm taking advantage of Mark.

You can't compare the two, Chris says. In no way can you compare the two.

Still, the power feels uncomfortable. I can scrutinise the transcript and emails, criticise his answers and observations. Take his latest email:

I was unhappy as a child, and then as a teenager, and I erected the most impregnable emotional barriers I could muster in what amounted to

137

desperate self-preservation. I was determined that no one and nothing be able to reach the parts of me that could be hurt, ever again. My chief weapons were bitter cynicism, and a biting, cruel sarcasm, which I cultivated with great diligence. I always felt that, to some degree, you could see through most of that, to the mostly terrified teenage boy at war with himself and trying desperately to make sense of the world.

Is he writing jacket copy for the book he imagines? Also: *barriers, weapons, and war?* We need to use the phone.

'You have him on tape admitting to the crime,' Chris says. 'What if you handed it over to the police? You could find out how law enforcement reacts.'

'No, I tell him. No. I wouldn't do that. I'd never do that. I told Mark—'

'Just hear me out,' Chris says. 'A lot of these guys don't get punished.'

'But this happened fourteen years ago. That's not to say there should be a time limit, but in this instance he's expressed remorse.'

'But think of what a great ending it would be.'

'You're joking,' I say.

'Yeah, sort of.'

'I won't do it.'

'And then, reader,' Chris says, 'I had him arrested.'

I tell my editor about what Chris said.

'It's funny,' she says, 'but there's truth in it too. Why wouldn't you have Mark arrested? I mean, it makes sense why you wouldn't. But how would you articulate your reasons?'

'Him getting arrested wouldn't make me feel any better,' I tell her, 'and I really don't think he'd do something like this again. And also, I don't want to put myself through the experience of reporting him. Oh, what do you think of *Reader, I Had Him Arrested*, as a chapter heading?'

'I think it carries too much shock value,' she says.

'OK.'

'But why does it carry too much shock value?' she asks. 'Why should the reader be shocked? Never mind. I think you should keep it. If the reader feels shocked, then that's good.'

EQUAL AND OPPOSITE

I lie awake thinking of Hannah, remembering the last time we met. It was finals week, and we were in my office, discussing all the books we'd read that semester.

'I like that we didn't read any men,' she told me.

'I figure you get enough of them in your other classes,' I said.

I could tell she was stressed, but I didn't think she needed the campus health centre. She needed one less final to worry about.

'Congratulations,' I told her after our hour-long meeting.

'What do you mean?'

'You just earned an A on the final.'

As far as I was concerned, she'd aced the exam.

'You don't know how much this means to me,' she said.

We made plans to meet after the holidays.

I return to my comments on an early draft of her essay. I wrote *Phenomenal.* I suggested cutting this line: *A grown woman, now—or growing still—who has survived so much and still has so much to survive.* It seemed too sentimental. But so what? Isn't that better than what I'm doing? I can feel myself, at times in this project, showing off. Here, an example: Newton's third law of motion says that when one body exerts a force on a second body, the second body simultaneously exerts a force equal in magnitude and opposite in direction on the first body.

But I just lay there.

I wonder if this book is exerting force back on Mark. I feel it exerting its force back on me.

I remember Mark comforting me after a physics exam, 'It's just Newtonian mechanics.'

YOU ALSO APOLOGISE TO BUGS

Chris and I are on our couch, grading student essays. I encounter another essay about rape.

'The student, she seems to blame herself for the rape,' I tell Chris. 'It happened when she was in high school. Her friend's brother did it, and I just, I don't know.'

He suggests we stop grading, do some work in the yard.

'No,' I tell him. 'I need to finish this stack of essays. I'm so behind.'

He puts his arm around me.

'You get the gardening stuff,' I say. 'I'll join you in a bit.'

But instead of grading, I surprise myself by drafting a list of What Else There Is to Do Before Calling Mark Again: review Ohio sexual assault statistics from 2003, interview somebody in the FBI about the revised definition of rape, research the history of feminist law reform—

Somebody knocks at the front door. I open it, and Chris is there.

'Come on,' he says and hands me a shovel. 'Help me in the garden.'

While we dig holes for new plants I tell him, 'I regret not telling Mark that I recorded our call.'

'You told him you're writing a book,' Chris says.

'I know,' I say. 'You're right.'

And then, in an effort not to kill any worms, I take breaks to move them gently off to the side.

'Sorry, worm,' I say each time.

Chris laughs.

'You do apologise too much,' he says.

In bed I tell Chris, 'You also apologise to bugs. I've heard you. Just last week, you apologised to dead ants caught in a trap.'

'That's probably because I spend so much time with you,' he says.

I wake up at 5:00 a.m., and I realise what must be so obvious: by never allowing myself to feel angry at Mark, I forgave him easily—but even to say I forgave him insults the very concept of forgiveness. I forgave him when I had no anger, loathing, hatred, resentment, or contempt to overcome.

I schedule an extra therapy appointment with Adam.

Adam asks me, 'What would it be like to have Mark experience shame and for you to not necessarily do anything?'

'Do anything as in—'

'That impulse where you feel like you need to do something. In other words, *Now that he feels shame, that must mean that I'm supposed to forgive him.* That's an impulse. That's a reaction.'

'OK, but then this is tricky. Because I don't know how reactive I'm being. I've been reading some philosophy texts on forgiveness. So I don't know how much of an impulse it is to forgive, if I'm reading about forgiveness. Do you know what I mean?'

Adam says, 'As I'm listening, what I'm hearing is— although it's good to get more information—is this another way, perhaps, to bypass feeling a feeling?'

'I think the anger is there. I think I feel uncomfortable saying it's there—because there is this gendered component.'

'Am I mansplaining?' Adam asks me, and I laugh.

'No, you're my therapist,' I tell him. 'I want your take.'

LOCKED IN THE SIXTEENTH CENTURY

For the next two weeks, I print academic articles and staple. Print and staple.

I highlight *Prosecutions are most likely to succeed when the victim can be considered as property herself. In the home counties between 1558 and 1599, the only convictions that were imposed were on men accused of raping young girls.*

I highlight Saint Albert the Great's no-means-yes claim: *As I heard in the confessional in Cologne, delicate wooers seduce women with careful touches. The more these women seem to reject them, the more they really long for them and resolve to consent to them. But in order to appear chaste, they act as if they disapprove of such things.*

I highlight *Rape of a virgin, a young woman, was regarded as the theft of her virginity, the property of her father to be used in procuring an advantageous marriage.*

So, my nineteen-year-old mindset was locked in the sixteenth century: at least the assault happened after my dad died— because then I didn't have to worry about hurting my dad.

I take an ibuprofen. This headache is not going away.

After a memoir about grief and mental illness, and now a memoir about sexual assault, I am definitely doing something light next time. Maybe a children's book featuring my cats. *Wet Nose on My Toes?*

'Flannery and Bishop,' I tell Chris, 'aren't mentioned in the book as much as they probably should be.'

'They won't know,' he says.

'But it seems wrong not to include them more,' I tell him. 'Bishop sits on my lap while I write in my room. Flannery sits next to me while I read on the couch. They sleep with us. We are with them all the time.'

'You can't include everything,' he says.

This book is making me insane, or: I am insane for writing it.

I open my fridge and stare, which is what I do whenever I feel stuck with writing.

I am one of those people who (if there are such people) delay opening their fancier perishable food—kalamata olive hummus, for example—until one day they realise it's two months expired. There's a moral there, I think.

It's time to call Mark.

FINDING EQUIVALENCES

I called Mark, and as soon as I heard his voice, I felt nostalgic for our friendship. I know, I just know, that I was too nice again.

I don't want to transcribe the call.

I share the phone transcript—of my first conversation with Mark—with Sarah.

'Do you notice how he's always finding equivalences for the two of you?' she asks me. 'It reads like a really underhanded way of minimising his actions.'

'I don't know if I follow,' I tell her.

'When he said that you were both drunk—without mentioning that only one assaulted the other. And when you said you didn't think the friendship could survive, he said, *I felt the same way*. How could he possibly have felt the same way as you about anything in relation to the assault?'

'Well, that was in regard to the friendship not surviving,' I tell her. 'That makes sense, that he would feel that way, that it couldn't survive.'

'What about the part when he said, *We were coming from very similar places. We were both incredibly depressed?*'

'OK, you're right,' I tell her. 'I hadn't noticed any of that.'

'And think about how the conversation ends with him saying *Anything I can do*. He's got the power. Again. And I think this process needs unpacking at some point—this impulse that seems to rule over you in the conversation, to move yourself out of the power position. And how he is involved in that.'

'You're so good,' I tell her. 'I hadn't considered him taking power when he said that. I thought, *Oh, he's being really nice.*'

'On one level he is, but there's the other level—if he is helping you, then he again has the power. To give and withhold. You are the supplicant then. It is really, really, really baroque and convoluted and cool. I think there's something fascinating about how every time you talk about helping him, I just want to say, Stop, stop, stop, stop. Which I think is great that the reader has that experience. But eventually, I want the memoirist to know at least as much as I do.'

At the risk of sounding sentimental, here's what I'm learning: this book isn't just about my friendship with Mark. It's about my friendships with other women.

I wish I'd shared the first transcript with Sarah before calling Mark again.

...

M E: I just want to give you a heads-up that I'm taping this.
HIM : That's fine.
M E: I've been thinking a lot about our last phone call. You mentioned that you briefly had a therapist.
HIM : Yeah, for a few months. Would have been after I dropped out of college.
M E: Did you ever tell your therapist about what happened between us?
HIM : No, but I need to tell—I haven't told anybody. I've been sort of locked in my own head on this—because I feel like I need another person that's not you to talk with about this and I don't have that person.
M E: Sure.

HIM : There are some things that—it feels unfair. Like, you're not my therapist.

M E: Unfair to whom?

HIM : I feel it's unfair of me to ask you to—maybe I'm just overthinking it.

M E: You mean you think it's unfair for you to talk about it to me.

HIM : Not so much about it, but—I don't know how interesting my own guilt and my own process with that is from your position.

M E: I recognise that the dynamic here is really messed up.

HIM : The whole situation is a little fraught.

M E: Definitely. So you never told your therapist. A lot of therapists don't even want to talk to perpetrators. Everyone wants to treat who they perceive as the clear victims.

HIM : Right. I can see that.

M E: And so it actually makes it really difficult to address sexual assault as the giant problem that it is. I was at a party a few months ago, and I found myself saying: *Look, I'm not defending paedophilia, but...* Which is not really a good conversation starter at a party. The problem is, there's not much in place for paedophiles to seek treatment. There was this great This American Life segment on a guy who identified as a paedophile but had never acted on his impulses. He tried to get help from therapists, but every therapist he tried rejected him after they found out what he was there for.

HIM : I've never attempted to get a therapist. But it's tough to, I don't know—how do you introduce yourself to somebody: *So, when I was nineteen, I sexually assaulted my best friend.*

M E: So you haven't talked about it with anyone at all?

HIM : Right. Which is sort of my process on a lot of things.

AND NEVER MIND

Mark said he needs to tell somebody about this—somebody who's not me. And yet he also said that he likely won't tell anybody.

And there are so many sliding-scale therapists where he lives. I know, because I just searched for sliding-scale therapists within a fifteen-mile radius of where he works. I could call a few, just to see if they'd be willing to talk with a perpetrator of sexual assault. Then, if they are agreeable, I could share their contact information with Mark.

I imagine what Sarah would say, and never mind. Her cerebral cortex would explode. Mark can make the calls.

...

M E: You mentioned last time that your sister knows, or knew, what happened between us.

HIM: She knew other people who were at that party. You'd have to talk to her about the sequence of events, but she—she was mad at me at the time about it. I don't know how much detail she knows, but she knows something happened.

M E: You and Jake, did you never discuss that night? You guys were living together. But he never talked about it with you?

HIM : No, I mean, obviously he knew that something had happened, but no, we never had a real conversation about it. I cut him pretty much completely out of my life years and years ago.

M E: Last time we talked, you mentioned that if we hadn't been in that basement—but then I got to thinking, Why was I taken to the basement?

HIM : I don't know, honestly, offhand. Probably I suggested it, but I don't know.

M E: I barely remember the house.

HIM : The basement was my room.

M E: I had gone through the rest of the house, because Jake's uncle was proud of certain rooms. He held open a *Playboy* for me, and I was like, Cool.

HIM : That sounds like him.

M E: Already, within fifteen minutes of meeting him, he was talking about a woman on a scale of one to ten.

HIM : That also sounds like him. He's kind of a pig.

M E: I vaguely remember the house, but I remember the first floor, where the party was, seemed pretty big. There were other rooms you could have taken me to. That's why I'm asking, Why the basement?

HIM : We used to hang out down there because there was a big double sectional couch and I had my computer set up with speakers. So we would hang out down there and get stoned.

M E: You and Jake?

HIM : Not so much me and Jake. But at parties people would bring weed.

M E: I was fall-down drunk, and then to go down all those stairs. That's what doesn't make sense. So you're not sure if you suggested it?

HIM : No, I'm not.

M E: What did the basement look like? I don't remember if there were posters, or if there was a twin bed.

HIM : I think I had a full-size bed. The way the basement was laid out, you came down a straight set of stairs from the hallway on the ground floor, and then my bed was tucked around an area beside those stairs. If you went down those stairs and immediately turned around, that's where the bed was. And then in front of the stairs, when you got to the bottom of them, there was that big L-shaped sectional down there and I had my computer desk set up facing it so you could watch a movie from the couch.

ME: I think I had only visited that house the once. That was the only time. You've thought about that night, about what happened, over the years. How frequently would you say?

HIM : I mean, it's the biggest regret of my life. When I get low, I get preoccupied by it.

THE BIGGEST REGRET OF MY LIFE

Good, the assault should preoccupy him.

...

M E: What has your dating life been like since then? Do you think it's affected how you—

HIM : I mean, I really, I basically don't have a social life. I really have never seriously dated.

M E: Had you been with anyone before that night? Had you ever—

HIM : I figured we would get here eventually, but I'm like the forty-year-old virgin.

M E: So you have never had sex with anyone. OK, so then—

HIM : Which is also something I don't really talk about with people.

M E: Sure, sure. I can understand. Do you—I can't believe these are some of the questions that I'm immediately cutting into. I'm sorry, but—

HIM : I'm sure this is one of those things that will feel healthy in retrospect.

M E: Tie feelings to events. I've looked into this. You're not supposed to recount just events, or just feelings. You're supposed to do both. That's supposed to be healthy. Anyway. This is a—whatever, I'll ask it: what kind of porn did you watch in high school, and did it ever portray non-consensual sex? And do you think porn affected your approach to the assault? Did it affect why you stopped when you did? I'm thinking about the experience of porn: where you're masturbating to an image. Do you know what I mean?

HIM : I watched porn, but I wasn't watching simulated rapes, if that's what you're getting at.

M E: I'm not judging. I'm also not trying to be reductive and arguing that porn leads to this, or anything like that. I guess I'm just curious. If you feel comfortable answering. I remember, by the way, when you accidentally stole a *Playboy* from the drugstore.

HIM : OK, there are two aspects of that that are wrong. It's that it wasn't a *Playboy*. It was the *Sports Illustrated* Swimsuit Issue. And it wasn't so much accidental as I just said it was accidental and I really was just stealing it. I went through a little phase when I was a kid. I started stealing little stuff just to see if I could.

M E: I remember us all making fun of you for that.

HIM : I was banned from—it was super embarrassing— but I was banned from Drug Mart until I was twenty-one. I actually didn't go back in until I was twenty-one.

YOU ALWAYS FIND A WAY TO LASH YOURSELF

At therapy I tell Adam, Because it didn't seem a clean, clearcut instance of rape, I couldn't see the situation according to good or evil. I think that's the hard part. That's what makes me really angry. Because I think of what Mark recently told me—about how ever since he was a little kid, he would steal things, little things, just to see what he could get away with. Obviously, there's that parallel: what can he get away with? If you keep doing these little things, in some ways, it seems so much more manipulative. I'm glad he didn't go further, but there's part of me that thinks, had he gone further, I would have known how to feel. Does that make sense?

So when you have that moment, Adam says, where you think, *Knowing what I know, knowing a little bit more about him now, that feels manipulative*, is there another feeling for you that goes along with that?

I'm angry at myself. I'm angry that I was so naive. Angry that I let him get away with it. What makes me really angry is that we were really good friends. He also knew I was upset about my dad. And he knew something had happened with my newspaper adviser.

Why is all the anger at you? Adam asks.

You tell me, I say.

I can. But in one respect I wanted to throw a little party here in New Jersey after you said you were angry at yourself. So there is anger. Right? Why you? That Mark betrayed you or turned on you, it's almost as if that can't stand alone. But now, *When I think about him and this and that, I can understand where he came from.* But there's that third thing where: *I'm done being angry at myself. You fucking did this to me. I thought I was in a safe place. I was with all friends and I was drunk, and you did this. You're an asshole.* Where is that?'

'It's weird to suddenly feel anger about something that happened fourteen years ago,' I say. 'Because anger is usually something you feel immediately. And so now I think, *Well, that's immature of me. Fourteen years have passed.*'

'You're incorrigible,' Adam says. 'You always find a way to lash yourself.'

'Because,' I reply, 'I went on for weeks, *I don't know why I can't feel anger*, and now I feel a lot more aware of my anger. I mean, here's this guy who stole things just to see what he could get away with. Meanwhile, I've always worked so hard. And I don't like that I'm pointing back at me, thinking, *Well, I worked so hard.* I'm mad that a lot of white middle-class guys like Mark have the luxury to not work very hard and still do OK. It makes me so angry that these guys can get away with so much.'

And yet, I won't report Mark to the authorities—even though I now have proof.

...

M E: So porn then, porn wasn't—the porn you watched was just basic porn? I don't even know what basic porn would be.

HIM: Yeah, I got in trouble a couple times in high school about Internet porn. I got caught.

M E: By your parents?

HIM: Yeah. [We laugh.]

M E: That's embarrassing. In the act of watching?

HIM : No, I'd save videos or whatever and my dad would find them. Or they'd be in the browsing history.

M E: So with your dad, did he ever sit you and your siblings down? Did he and your mom ever talk about sex?

HIM : Neither one of them is very good about talking about that. My dad would do the I'm not mad, I'm just disappointed thing, but they'd also guilt-trip me about how he's a junior high principal. Just like how it was irresponsible of me because it was putting his standing with the school board at risk if anybody found out. Caesar's wife must be above reproach. That sort of thing.

M E: But they never talked to you about sex?

HIM : I don't really recall a serious conversation with my parents.

M E: So then this is kind of interesting to me as a writer, and also, just so you know, enough time has passed and I'm able to approach this from a remove. I'm OK.

HIM : That's good. It's healthy. It's good to hear that.

M E: It's interesting because there was a new definition of rape that the FBI put forth in 2013. Prior to that it was very antiquated: the carnal knowledge of a female, forcibly and against her will.

HIM : That was the legalistic language?

M E: Yeah, yeah, within the FBI's Uniform Crime Reporting Summary Reporting System, that's what rape was. And that went unchanged since 1927. But then, in 2013, the FBI updated the definition, and that was actually under Director Mueller. The new definition is the penetration, no matter how slight, of the vagina or anus with any body part or object, or oral penetration by a sex organ of another person, without the consent of the victim. So what's interesting to me is that the actions are the same. In 2003, what happened between us was sexual assault, but now, according to legal terms, what happened would be rape. I'm interested in how we assign or categorise human behaviour. I don't know. What do you think of that?

HIM : I couldn't have told you that that was a thing. I'm sort of processing being, legally speaking, a rapist. Which I'm not proud of. Yeah. So, which I guess is fair.

M E: It's interesting to me because I, for so long, had trouble considering what had happened, what you had done, as—well, I didn't want to think about it or talk to therapists about it because I didn't want to jeopardise my intense grief for my dad. I thought that if I told a therapist, they would focus on this. Because everyone seemed to think I was grieving for my dad for an unreasonably long time. They didn't think my grief made sense.

HIM : Yeah, and the rape is not what you want to actually talk about.

UP TO MARK?

When Mark used the word *rape*, I felt uncomfortable instead of vindicated. I think that's because *sexual assault* (and sometimes I even drop the *sexual*) allows me to ignore the particulars. The particulars: someone suggested (likely Mark) that I should be carried from the living room into Mark's basement room; Mark and Jake carried me into Mark's basement room; Mark told Jake that Jake could leave; after Jake left, Mark undressed me; Mark put his fingers inside my vagina as far as they would go; I cried and Mark told me not to cry; Mark told me I was dreaming; Mark took his fingers out of me and masturbated over me.

Why would Jake have suggested Mark's basement room? I can almost hear Mark suggesting it. But I can't offer proof, and I feel so much pressure to provide proof, which is why I'm interviewing Mark. Yet why should the proof be up to Mark? Why should he get to decide what happened? I think of the detectives saying, Is it possible that his hand slipped? My newspaper adviser never admitted to rubbing his hand up my thigh and between my legs.

But Mark admitted to assaulting me, to *sexually* assaulting me.

Mark admitted to raping me.

. . .

M E: I also had trouble deciding whether it was a big deal.

HIM : I can understand—well, I should let you finish, but I can understand why you would process it in that way, and it just makes me sad. The whole thing just—

M E: I think I'm OK now. But I was thinking about this new definition and I realised that the reason I had trouble even thinking of it as rape, or even serious, was, Well, he used his fingers, and it wasn't violent. We're so used to movie portrayals of violent rape, usually followed by murder, and we barely learn who the woman was. Then I realised I was so focused on thinking about your body, your hands, whatever was being used, that I wasn't thinking about my body. I was only thinking about what it meant for the perpetrator, and what the perpetrator used, instead of thinking about it from the other point of view.

HIM : Well, hopefully you're not thinking that way anymore.

M E: No, but you know, after encountering the new definition, in some way—it's sort of silly, but now I can say it was serious.

HIM : I don't think it's silly at all. I think that's why it's important that our laws reflect society and reality as best as they can. I don't know exactly what I'm trying to articulate here, but that is one of the functions of useful laws, to give us a framework by which to form a collective society, to understand these are the boundaries and this is what is not OK.

M E: I do think structural change happens through laws. Because a lot of people won't take some actions seriously if the law doesn't categorise them as such. I was recently thinking about popular movie portrayals of rape. Movies that came out when we were kids. There isn't a lot of nuance in these movies. I'm thinking of Sally Field in *Eye for an Eye*, avenging her daughter's rape and murder. At least it's a woman avenging a rape. But it's pretty simplistic.

HIM : Vengeance is easy to sell.

M E: It's why so many people love *The Godfather*. Vengeance and supposedly family values. I was also thinking about things I heard when I was a teenager. Women just aren't as funny as men. Or, women just can't do math and science as well as men. Things like that. I'm wondering—not whether you bought into that—but if you remember those generalisations.

HIM : I don't think I personally felt that way. I certainly don't now. I don't feel like I had trouble accepting that women were intelligent on their own merits.

M E: Sure, I just mean like the general mood in Sandusky, Ohio.

HIM : Yeah, that as a backdrop, you're dead on that that was a thing.

M E: I remember Jake explaining to me—Jake loved to explain things.

HIM : Yeah, mostly badly. [We laugh.]

M E: Yeah, he would explain women weren't as funny. I mean, he was in high school. His views have probably changed. And it's interesting to think about the kids who are growing up with the #MeToo movement, and it's so much more in the national discourse.

HIM : When we were in high school, feminism felt like a thing that had already happened. And like we had kind of gotten somewhere halfway around equality.

M E: Right.

HIM : But it had kind of stopped. Which, yeah, is certainly not the mood now. Yeah, the #MeToo movement happening concurrently with these conversations is, I don't know, fitting. Not the easiest thing. It's just every time I see a #MeToo story, it's just like it's Me… too.

HE TOLD YOU THAT?

I ask Chris how he feels about my talking to Mark.

I don't like him for what he did, Chris says. Plenty of nerdy teenage boys are frustrated sexually but don't assault someone. I was a pudgy kid in high school and frustrated that I didn't have a girlfriend. I had a lot of friends who were girls. On school camping trips, some of the girls would want to share a tent with me. I remember this one girl saying, I'm going to cuddle with Chris. But I never ever—

It wouldn't have occurred to you, I tell him.

No. Of course not. That's not what you do.

A lot of people aren't going to like what I'm doing, giving him a voice.

Don't think about that, Chris says. Not right now, anyway.

Do you think I care too much about what people think, and that's why I forgave Mark?

No. I think you just look for the good in people. And he was your best friend. He wasn't some stranger.

That's what makes this so hard.

And interesting, Chris says.

Yeah. We're not in some clichéd movie. I'm not some anonymous woman who gets two minutes of screen time before she's raped and murdered by a stranger. But I do feel bad for not feeling how I think I'm supposed to feel. Really, I feel bad for him. He said it was the biggest regret of his life. He doesn't really have any friends. He's never had a girlfriend. He's still a virgin.

He told you that?

Yeah. I actually think these phone calls are helping him. Here I was worried about his mental health. But he's opening up, says it feels good to do.

You were laughing while you were on the phone with him. Did that upset you?

Kind of. I had to leave the house, go for a walk. I hate him for what he did to you.

...

M E: I don't know if I would have decided to pursue this if not for #MeToo. I support the movement. But as someone who identifies as a feminist, I feel conflicted because the narrative I feel like I'm supposed to assume, I'm supposed to hate you—

HIM : Right. And it'd be easier in a lot of ways—I think for me, even—if it was like, She hates me now and this is this terrible thing that I did. The forgiveness or attempted forgiveness or whatever you want to call it, it's welcome but it's tricky to process.

M E: Just because—

HIM : Because I never forgave myself, so it's weird. It's just strange to me, that you have.

M E: So, what happened, you've never done anything like that to anyone else?

HIM : No. Which I don't know if that makes it better or worse.

M E: It's interesting because I was reading textbooks on perpetrators and the common traits of victims. The victims tend to be open-minded. They're often in a state of vulnerability. Perpetrators will often choose a victim based on the victim's good qualities or other characteristics, such as being polite, giving people the benefit of the doubt, being trusting, being shy, vulnerable, or accessible. And I do like to give people the benefit of the doubt. But I don't like to see my behaviour in the context of a textbook. In some ways it can be reassuring, but in other ways, I don't know.

HIM : Sure. You are your own individual, not limited to the textbook descriptions of your behaviour.

M E: Right. The word you used earlier, fraught, this whole thing is very fraught for me. And even thinking about all of this and—by giving you the benefit of the doubt and forgiving you and believing it's possible to be a good person and make a mistake. I don't know. I feel like a terrible feminist. Progressives, we will set up non-profit organisations to deliver books to prisoners, prisoners who may have raped and murdered, and I'm not disagreeing with delivering books to prisoners. But I guess I'm confused about where the empathy is sometimes allowed to go.

HIM : That's kind of an interesting point. Because in progressive circles, there is an expectation to vilify certain behaviours and people, and how you get from one category to another is sometimes more complicated than we would like it to be.

M E: It is very confusing. So you had thought all these years that I hated you?

HIM : Well, I mean—at least that you should.

M E: So immediately you felt—when did you start to regret it?

HIM : It was one of those things where I knew while I was doing it that I shouldn't be doing it, and I just did it anyway. It was strange.

WRESTLING WITH THIS STUFF

Rebekah calls me, wants to know how the latest call went.

If Mark were a meathead, I tell her, if Mark were a bro-y guy, if Mark hadn't given me exactly what I needed, then I would have an easier time feeling anger. And he was reflective about his role in the #MeToo movement. Also, he doesn't occupy some high-up position. He doesn't really have friends. Maybe he's living the life he wants to be living, but he also seems kind of sad and depressed and lonely. And so I have a hard time accessing anger.

Your description of the guy, Rebekah says, I mean my God. I would be wrestling with this stuff too.

Really? I ask her.

Absolutely.

That makes me feel better, I tell her. And you know, I think it's easy to hate someone who's successful and is horrible to women. If Mark didn't feel remorse, this wouldn't be as interesting to me.

This is the thing that makes the story unique, she says. The story is worth telling regardless, but this is what sets it apart. It's participating in the #MeToo genre, but also is saying something a little bit different or a little bit new. I'm excited about this for the very reasons that you're feeling trepidation.

...

M E: When did you feel that the friendship between us was coming apart?

HIM: It was never really the same after that, right? We did talk afterwards. I think basically at the time we decided to try to ignore the problem. I was never really successful in that.

M E: I don't remember how things dissipated.

HIM: Part of that was we were high school friends that went to college in different cities. We didn't see each other that much, and I don't think—it was hard—it would have been hard for me to—I don't know. I was so ashamed of myself I didn't—I didn't want the reminder of what had happened is, I think, a large part of the reason why I didn't try harder to keep the friendship alive.

THE ASSAULT HAD CHANGED

In the weeks after the assault, I found it strange that I could answer Mark's calls in my normal voice. Was I forcing my voice to sound as it did before, or was my voice telling me that the assault had changed, or should change, nothing between us?

And my voice now? I'm still speaking to him as if I'm over the assault. I even told him, *Enough time has passed and I'm able to approach this from a remove. I'm OK.*

Chris is on the couch, reading poetry. Flannery is snoring next to him.

Am I genuine? I ask him.

What? he says.

I'm being nice to Mark on the phone, but really I'm manipulating him.

You told him you're writing a book, Chris reminds me. Mark knows that.

But I'm talking to him as if I'm OK. I also said I'd run the manuscript by him. I can't do that. But I just blurted it out.

Don't show it to him, Chris says.

Mark did say that he's not trying to limit what I'm trying to do. I don't think he really expects me to run it by him. Maybe I should get tattoo sleeves.

What?

Like those punk girls at the vegan diner, I explain. Girls with sleeves don't put up with anything, you know?

This morning I woke up with my fists clenched and my head far away, back to high school, to Mark's house, to video games and physics formulas, to leftover Halloween candy and laughter about a hell house.

I email Mark, asking him for five good memories. I want him to remember more than the assault—because I want to believe our friendship mattered.

...

M E: Do you think the fact that I was—I mean, it was the first time I'd ever been drunk. Do you think beyond the fact that I was really drunk and couldn't consent—do you think that because I was at a school in another city—I don't know how much rationalisation crossed your mind, but back then did you think that you wouldn't see me much, and therefore—

HIM : I think it was more of being presented with that opportunity in that state—that there was just a momentary lapse of whatever you'd call it: self-control, decency.

M E: So you don't remember whose suggestion it was to take me into the basement?

HIM : I wish I did but no.

M E: Do you think Jake knew? You know how sometimes guys will—if they think, These two will finally get together, I'm just going to peace out and leave them alone. Do you think Jake was—

HIM : I don't really think so. I think that something had happened came to him as a surprise the next morning, if I'm recalling correctly.

M E: And then he never addressed it.

HIM : No, I mean he knew I was upset and you were— that something had happened, but I don't think we ever talked in any detail about what had happened.

M E: Within our friend circle, how much did you open up with others—not about this but with your emotions in general?

HIM : You were the only one I ever really talked to about much of anything that mattered. I've not really ever made friends that way. I don't know. We used to talk a lot. I mean there were a couple of semesters there when we were talking for hours. Which I didn't really do with anybody else.

M E: And you remember—I was having such a hard time that there are huge gaps in my memory from college. Do you—what do you remember of me? That's a pretty self-involved question. But did I talk a lot about my dad?

HIM : I just remember we were both having a really hard go of it for a while. Because we had started talking more on the phone before your dad had died. I knew you were having a really hard time dealing with it, but I didn't know the extent to which you were having a hard time dealing with it. It seemed like you were struggling because you had gone originally as a journalism student. It seemed like you were wanting to pursue creative writing, and that was a source of frustration. And then your boyfriend was a source of frustration. And then your dad died. And obviously everything that goes along with that. I remember these long, sad phone calls. But at the same time those are good memories for me. Because I was in similar headspaces if not lower, and just to connect with somebody felt good.

I WAS IN A WORSE PLACE

When Mark ranked his pain, I instantly thought, *No, I was in a worse place. I was depressed. My dad died.* But maybe Mark did feel just as sad or sadder. Depression isn't necessarily caused by an event. Still, I'm mad at him for saying that. Sarah's right: he kept equalising our experiences.

...

M E: I remember feeling conflicted about the journalism school because I felt I was only there because I'd been editor of the high school paper, and the only reason I'd been editor was, I thought, because my newspaper adviser was a creep. His harassing me, it went on for a long time.

HIM: That's tough. You didn't ever talk about being assaulted in high school. I don't think we ever—that was all rumours that ever got to me at the time. Which I can understand not wanting to talk about it.

M E: One of the big questions I've had over the years is why did you stop when you did? Why—

HIM: You know, I've asked myself that question a lot, and honestly I think I just chickened out. And I'm glad I did, but—

M E: Why do you think that is? Because you hadn't been with a girl prior?

HIM: No, I mean—I think it was the kind of thing where I knew I shouldn't be doing it.

M E: And so there was a line—

HIM : That was apparently as far as I was willing to transgress on that particular night.

NOT AN EASY THING FOR PEOPLE TO COUGH UP

Every day the past week, I worry that I forgot to turn off the stove. To lock the door. Before I leave the house, I take my keys out of my bag, put them back in, and take them out—at least three times. As I do this, I notice my knuckles have started to bleed.

How often are you washing your hands? Chris asks.

Only as much as I need to, I say.

Jung and I get drinks. She asks me, Are you looking out for yourself? It sounds like it could be emotionally difficult.

I have a good therapist, I tell her.

This morning I woke up to Mark, the figment of Mark, standing over me, like he was right there. I looked down. My clothes were on me. I looked up. Mark was gone.

I arrange to meet with Adam twice a week.

I tell Adam, I'm taking Mark at his word. He said he's never done it again. And he was never a really social guy, and so I don't think he's put himself in the position to do it again. But if given the opportunity, would he do it again? I don't know. Maybe he only did it once.

I've talked to enough people, Adam says, where it's usually not the case. I have people who feel very comfortable in here telling me about one thing that happened one time, and then two years later they'll tell me about this other thing. It's not an easy thing for people to cough up.

So it's not a one-off, right? Statistically.

No.

I know you're not seeing him, so how can you guess or know. I just wonder. His psychology is such that he used to see what he could get away with. But he has been depressed, and so he doesn't socialise.

He may have sublimated his urges by getting sex workers, Adam says. When I picture him from your descriptions, I picture him very alone and reclusive and, in this day and age, probably finding ways to have sex with himself on the computer. I picture him in his living room just finding ways to—he doesn't feel good after it—but finding ways not to do the wrong thing. But he definitely doesn't feel right about it.

...

M E: What do you remember of the morning after?

HIM : I remember I was kind of—when I'm really upset, basically what I do is kind of stew motionlessly, and I just get kind of deep in my own head. So I was doing that. And then Jake at some point had found out that something had happened. He came downstairs to check on me, to make sure I wasn't—he was surprised. He wanted to make sure I wasn't going to start throwing things and breaking things. Which I didn't.

M E: Is that what he said?

HIM : That's basically what he was concerned about. But yeah, I don't really—I remember—I wish I remembered more. I think it was a couple of days—it wasn't that day—it was a couple of days later by the time—probably you worked up the nerve to call me. I don't think it was the other way around. I'm sure I didn't.

M E: I think I remember you calling me.

HIM : Maybe I did.

M E: I think you did. And I was surprised. I wasn't expecting to hear from you again.

HIM : Understandably. Well, maybe I did work up the nerve then. It was one of those things—I felt terrible about it immediately, but you can't undo it.

M E: When you called me, I remember feeling really conflicted and partly—

HIM : I would have been mad at me.

M E: What's that?

HIM : I feel like if that had happened to me and then I called you two days later or whatever then I probably wouldn't have picked up the phone.

M E: I think I felt sort of—I wouldn't say happy. That's not quite right. I remember thinking, Maybe we can stay friends. It can be OK.

HIM : That's classic you.

M E: I'm like a dog. I just want everybody to like me.

HIM : That's such an unbelievably you reaction.

WHICH JUST CONFIRMS I'M USING HIM

Mark contradicted himself. In the first phone conversation, he said, *I remember doing that*, in reference to calling me after the assault. This time, he said, *I'm sure I didn't*, in reference to that call. I rack my brain for a coherent interpretation. Maybe, in the first conversation, he felt desperate to claim credit for doing something decent, such as taking the initiative to apologise—and this time he's careful not to take credit for a decent act that he potentially did not do.

I want to tell the truth, but I don't want to treat his answers as the absolute truth. The best I can figure: duplicity, intentional or not, is part of the human experience.

I'm three days into spring break, and I haven't left the house except to take out the recycling. In this time, I have suffered two nerdy injuries. The first: while standing on my toes to grab a novel from our topmost shelf, I knocked over a heavy bronze bookend and it fell onto my exposed shin. Blood ran down my shin and stained my new white sneakers. Well, just the right one. Now I can't wear skirts because it looks like I don't know how to shave my legs. The second injury: I stubbed my toe on my desk so badly that my toe started bleeding.

I probably should leave the house, but I want to finish transcribing my second phone conversation with Mark. Sarah calls, asks when I talk to him next.

I'm still working on part three, I tell her. Talking with him again, this soon, could screw up the section. Which just confirms that I'm using him.

You have to include that, Sarah says. The fact that you're using him belongs in there. Knowing that you're so conflicted about it.

I'm feeling less conflicted about it, I tell her.

That's what I want, she says, as a reader, for the character. I want her off of the circle of *is he a good person, is he not a good person*. I want him to become beside the point. I want him in the past. I want the narrator to reappropriate her own narrative. I want her to stop listening to him and recognise that in giving him so much voice, it's a re-enactment, in a way, of the rape. Where he talks more than she does.

I want that too.

...

M E: I think part of the reason I stopped talking with you is my college boyfriend didn't like the idea of my staying friends with you. He said, Jeannie, I can't forgive him. But I said, It's not for you to forgive. It happened to me. I was concerned if I stayed friends with you, or kept in touch with you, he would get mad and it'd ruin my relationship with him. I was just trying to make men happy. That was my life. So it's really—I distinctly remember, I think I told you last time, when we all went out for wings and my college boyfriend didn't want to go. Afterward, he said, I can't believe you made me do that. I find his response interesting.

HIM : It's like, what right do you have to be angry—

M E: Right. Which, I can understand it's a natural reaction.

HIM : Sure.

M E: I think everyone was confused about the situation, but I thought I was less confused than everyone else about the assault. I think of the idea of performing one's gender. It's not disingenuous because within the larger structural system we've been assigned these roles to play.

HIM: You feel it's expected of you.

M E: You feel it, or you've internalised it, and it often doesn't feel like performance to you, but it's also not completely genuine. I think I genuinely—I felt as if I'd genuinely forgiven you. I don't even know if I thought I had to forgive you. But I felt I had forgiven you. I don't know.

HIM: This is where you can get really reductive really quickly.

M E: Exactly. All I can say is how I remember feeling. And I did want our friendship to last, and honestly I think I was just having so many psychiatric problems that every relationship sort of died.

HIM: And I was in a bad place for other reasons. This just kind of exacerbated—the shame was kind of the cherry on top of the depression sandwich. You know I was miserable for a lot of my twenties, and this was a part of why but it's not the entire reason why. I don't want to give the impression that I'm blaming my rape of you for my own mental problems.

I THOUGHT I WAS LESS CONFUSED

I think everyone was confused about the situation, but I thought I was less confused than everyone else about the assault. I am so confused as to why I said that—seeing as how I didn't think our friends were really thinking about the assault. My college boyfriend was. I knew that much, because he expressed confusion and anger about my apparent lack of anger. I never should have insisted he meet Mark.

For my thirty-fourth birthday, Chris's mom mails me a mood ring.

This is so perfect, I tell Chris.

And I didn't even tell her, he says, that we'd been joking about this.

I put it on. According to the ring, I'm mad.

Two minutes later, I'm not.

A minute later, I am.

Now I'm not.

My adviser put his hand between my legs while I wore clothes.

Mark put his hand between my legs after he removed my clothes.

My other friend pinned me down and raped me after he removed my clothes.

I tell myself the progression is meaningless. Just a coincidence. I consult the ring. It's yellowish. According to the colour/mood chart, I feel either imaginative or unsettled mixed emotions. Is the ring questioning my memory, alleging that I'm imagining all of this? No, no, of course not. It's reassuring me that my emotions are indeed unsettled and mixed.

Now the ring is telling me I'm calm and relaxed. Either the ring is broken, or I'm broken. Or it's a novelty item and I should stop investing so much energy into analysing it.

Like me the night of the assault, the ring has no agency.

I wonder if Mark used me like a mood ring. Suddenly, he could see how angry he was. Angry about his virginity. So angry that he'd hurt one of his closest friends. It'd be easier to say that Mark wasn't thinking about my feelings that night. But I had been crying about my dad's death, crying about what my newspaper adviser had done to me. Mark, I'm sure, was thinking about my feelings. He selfishly used them to his advantage. I don't care if I don't have proof of his emotions that night.

I take off the ring. I'm mad.

...

M E: It's tricky. You're in a tough rhetorical position. This is a hypothetical, but if you had a son, how would you—I'm not saying come up with a solution, but I guess what do you think leads to teenage boys forgetting impulse control and making decisions like this?

HIM : I think part of it is unique to my own personal experience, but I think—let me see if I can come up with an answer here that makes any kind of rational sense. My family writ large does not communicate emotion well and my experience with it has been basically, Well, I'll not talk about it and not talk about it and not talk about it and not deal with something until it just erupts and then it's like a dam breaking and who knows what direction—who knows what collateral damage you'll get. So I think if I had a son, I would try to get him to be more open than I was, or am, and deal with his feelings and emotions directly. But I also don't plan on having children.

M E: Boys are often taught to suck it up and be a man, and I think of how damaging that has been for everyone involved. Do you also think—I mean, you and I were such good friends. Did any part of you feel like, I've been there for her so much, this was—

HIM : Well, I think what you're trying to ask me is did I think I deserved some sort of sexual accommodation, which, I don't really think so. I think definitely I wanted to figure out a way to move our relationship to an actual relationship and not just a friendship, but—

M E: You weren't sure how to express that.

HIM : Right. Because I couldn't even say, certainly at the time I couldn't even express, that I did like you in that way, let alone—I'm still not good at talking about it.

M E: It's hard to talk about. I'm asking you questions like, What sort of pornography did you watch in high school? and Did any of it portray non-consensual sex? It's OK.

HIM : I'll admit to having been a little caught off guard by that but it's not an unreasonable place to start.

M E: But you think a lot of it goes back to you didn't know how to express how you felt.

HOW MUCH MORE COULD YOU DO FOR HIM?

I'm mad at what Mark did, yet I want him to be OK. It's hard to feel contempt when for five years he was one of my closest friends.

Is there a possibility, Adam asks, that your project could be the very thing that would lead him to help?

Possibly, I say. A lot of my friends are surprised that he's agreed to talk. So maybe this is the first step.

I know I have the tendency to be a little protective of you, Adam says, but how much more could you do for him? This venue is a springboard for getting help. He's probably talked about this more in the past two months than he ever has. If he's ever talked about it at all. If things get kicked up, if he starts having bad dreams or intrusive thoughts, maybe he'll feel motivated to seek out help.

Maybe, I tell Adam. I hope.

I tell Sarah what Adam said.

Why is he engaging with you on this level of how to help Mark? she asks. Why isn't he guiding you to talk about your own experience?

He is, I tell her. I'm cherry-picking one conversation. But Adam is helping. It's just, I've been obsessing over whether I should help Mark find a therapist. Adam was responding to that.

You're not going to, are you?

No, no. I mean, he should do that. But therapy is expensive. I was just thinking I could find a sliding-scale therapist for him.

Stop worrying about him, she tells me.

My friend Tom calls, asks how this project is going.

It's OK, I tell him. Actually, it's not. I feel like I'll disappoint my friends—and women in general—by including so much of Mark's voice.

You're not going to please everybody, Tom says. And that's a good thing.

I wish I could think like that, I tell him.

A former war reporter, Tom now lives in Istanbul. Some years ago, masked men with Kalashnikovs captured him and other journalists in Aleppo. For reasons Tom still doesn't understand, his captors apologised, gave him and his colleagues lunch, bought them drinks at a roadside espresso stand, and released them hours later.

I ask him what he's working on, and he says he's compiling an oral history of ISIS.

You're interviewing ISIS? I say.

Through a network of Syrian fixers.

Wow, I say. That has got to be hard.

Yeah, he says. They've executed friends of mine. I don't agree with ISIS at all. But in order to fix a problem, you have to understand the enemy. What's interesting is not all of them execute people. Some are electricians responsible for keeping the grid on. Others distribute food and water to the locals. It's scary how nice some of these guys can seem. That's what makes it so insidious.

OK, I tell him. I feel so much better about my project.

ISIS and sexual abusers, Tom says. You might be in a slightly better position.

...

HIM : This is in one of the email drafts I deleted, but I distinctly remember telling myself—when I was in grade school probably—not to have emotions because that way the other kids in my class couldn't use them to hurt me, which is not really a productive way to go through life.

M E: Do you think you forgot that others have strong emotions?

HIM : It wasn't like I thought other people shouldn't have emotions. I didn't want to give anybody else anything that they could grab on to and use to hurt me.

M E: What were some of the thoughts that you had, or that you can recall having, that night? Either before or during or immediately after? I know you said you remember me crying. Do you remember what sort of thoughts were going through your mind?

HIM : I remember knowing that I shouldn't be doing this and doing it anyway. And then I remember you started to cry and then I lay down. There was a little gap where I lay down, and then I remember thinking maybe you were so drunk you wouldn't remember it, or that it was bad and then maybe it would be OK, and then you did start to cry and I remember you whispering, He raped me. And I realised that it wasn't going to be OK. And then it's just however many hours of just me realising what I had just done and that it wasn't going to be OK.

M E: It's strange to hear that I used that word rape, considering how I didn't think of it as rape at the time, or said I didn't think of it as rape. Did I just whisper that to no one?

HIM : Yeah, just, under your breath. I remember you were crying and said that. And yeah, it's tough really to think about.

SO WHY DO I STILL FEEL UNCOMFORTABLE?

Immediately after the assault happened, there, in the basement, with no one listening except for Mark, I whispered: he raped me. I don't remember this, but I believe Mark's memory. So why do I still feel uncomfortable using the word *rape*?

Mark is still him, regardless of what I call him.
And as for what he did—
Regardless of what I call it, his actions remain the same.

...

M E: Do you—have you thought about getting a therapist? Since we've started talking especially?
HIM : Have I thought about it? Sure. Am I at all likely to take the sort of action that leads to doing that? No.
M E: It's hard to find a good therapist.
HIM : It is, and like, I don't—like I said earlier, I could probably use somebody that's not you to talk about some of this stuff with, but my process is just more to not talk about it.
M E: Are you close friends with the guys you work with?
HIM : I was pretty good friends with a couple of the guys, but we've had some turnover. It's a really small business. It's mostly me and Sam. I like Sam fine and we

get along, but he's five years older and has a wife and three little girls. We don't hang out.

M E: So who do you spend time with then?

HIM : I sort of don't. I don't want to make myself out to be too much of a sad sack, but I really don't have a lot of close friends. I'm just bad at maintaining those relationships or starting new ones. It is sort of what it is.

M E: When you went back to college, to grad school, was it helpful taking classes with other people?

HIM : It was really helpful for me initially because it was good to have an excuse to think about—the kind of problems you have to do in engineering come pretty naturally to me. There's no non-braggart way to say this, but that kind of classwork is just not that hard for me. I can just sort of do it. It felt good to be back in that environment, to being the smart kid in the class. The math and physics of it is interesting to a certain extent, but I kind of realised that culturally I wasn't that interested in actually doing engineering. I don't have the part of me that wants to do six years of research. I'm not built to be an actual academic.

M E: Did you make many friends in grad school?

HIM : I would say I was friendly with my classmates. I kind of became friends with one of the guys, and then I was kind of shitty about it and just kind of ignored that relationship after we graduated.

M E: Why do you think that was?

HIM : I don't know. Part of it is I was trying to come to grips with, to come up to speed with the camera stuff, and my head just wasn't in the engineering stuff anymore. I'm bad at keeping friends around, which is really what it comes down to. I don't have that instinct that says to call up people because I haven't talked to them in a week or two weeks or month or whatever it is, and all of a sudden it's been three months and I haven't talked to the guy and now I feel like we're strangers.

M E: I can see how our friendship coming apart was hard for you. It was hard for me. But does it surprise you then that I don't feel enraged?

HIM : Yeah. I've been surprised by the extent to which you seem to have actually put it behind you and are engaging with it at a detached position, which I don't know if that's accurately describing how you're feeling. Like I said earlier, it'd be expected I guess and easier to navigate if you were just furious at me for the rest of time.

M E: Why do you think it would be easier to navigate? How would you navigate it then?

HIM : Obviously we wouldn't be having this conversation. It'd be like, I did a bad thing, and the person I did the bad thing to hates me now. I know what that is. That makes sense. It's unfortunate but the forgiveness is, like I said, it's great but it is more complicated. I feel like I have to have earned it, if that makes any sense, and I feel that I didn't.

M E: This makes me really happy, to talk with you again. Which is messed up probably, because I'm like, How nice it is of him to agree to talk to me. I'm recognising how complicated that is. I certainly had nightmares about what happened over the years. Conceptually, nightmares interest me because of the lack of consent that happens with nightmares.

HIM : Right. You can't opt out of the nightmare.

M E: To be sexually assaulted, that's really close to being a nightmare. You're usually in a bed, and you have no way of pushing the nightmare away. It's just going to happen.

HIM : There is some metaphor working overtime there.

IT'S JUST GOING TO HAPPEN?

Wait, what? By way of metaphor extension, I said of sexual assault, *It's just going to happen.*

I remember talking on the phone with my mom while walking to a subway station. I was in my early twenties, in Brooklyn, on my way to a date. A stranger grabbed me just as I was passing a dark alley.

What the fuck do you think you're doing? I shouted.

He ran off.

What happened? my mom asked. What's going on?

Some man grabbed me, I said, but he's gone now.

And now I'm remembering the guy who tried to undress me in his car. I had just moved to New York and was wandering through lower Manhattan on a hot summer evening. As I was passing an Italian restaurant, a man in the doorway stopped me, motioned me inside, said he needed customers so as to attract more customers.

I own the place, he said.

I almost suggested he take the Tony Soprano poster off the window, but I felt bad for him, thought, *Well, the rent here is pretty high.*

Drinks on me, he said.

I figured, *Why not? I can sit in the air-conditioning, drink for free, and read.* After a couple of hours of drinking and reading, I got up to leave and stumbled. How much wine had I drunk?

You're not taking the train home, are you? he asked.

Yeah, it's easy, I said.

But really I hated the idea of navigating the subway system drunk. I'd need to transfer trains at least once. And I didn't have enough money for a cab.

I'll drive you, he said.

So I followed him to his car, gave him my address, and tried not to throw up while he drove me to Brooklyn. I forget what we talked about on the way, but I remember feeling nervous and then reminding myself that he did own a restaurant—as if that reduced the likelihood he'd rape and/or murder me. He parked outside my apartment. I thanked him. But when I tried to open the passenger door, I couldn't. He pulled down the straps of my dress. I pushed him away and kept trying to unlock the door. He started kissing my neck and rubbing his hand up my thigh.

Don't you want to be pampered? he asked.

I took off my right shoe and stabbed its short heel into his thigh.

Hey! he shouted. I'm pampering you.

I pushed him, hit him, figured out the door, and ran half barefoot from the car to my apartment. He yelled, Goodnight, sweetheart!

Great, I thought. *Now he knows where I live.*

He called the next day, as if nothing had happened. He said he owned properties in Queens and Brooklyn and he'd rent a place to me at a good rate. I didn't remember giving him my number.

I don't think so, I said and hung up.

This is all to say: I could resist strangers, just not friends. Maybe because I figured I'd see Mark and my other friend again. And I did see them again, for a time.

Mark's comment about my nightmare metaphor *working over-time* really irritates me. I do think the shared setting of both experiences—Mark's assault of me and my nightmares about him—is interesting. Sure, comparing something terrible to a nightmare is trite. I guess I'll let myself be trite then.

...

ME: I think over the years, it certainly, what happened did impact the way I viewed men. The way I still view men.

HIM: I mean, it would have to, it seems like. I know it impacted—go ahead. I don't want to interrupt.

ME: It impacted how I felt about relationships, men, sex.

HIM: I can understand that totally. I felt similarly.

NO, YOU DID NOT FEEL SIMILARLY

No, no, no, he can't understand that totally. He did not feel similarly.

...

HIM : It led me to not really trust myself with women. I had done this thing, and I didn't really understand why.

ME: Do you think it's why you never—

HIM : I don't think it's the only reason why, but I'm sure it's a contributing factor. But by no means the only reason why.

ME: I always felt bad that I fell out of touch with your parents. I felt sick about it. I was sad because I missed all of you, but I wasn't going to explain to them why I disappeared. Do you talk to your parents regularly or see them regularly?

HIM : We have a decent relationship. I see them every few weeks to a month or so. They've been really supportive over the years financially, which has allowed me to be where I am now. Because basically they paid for my tuition to go back to grad school and I paid for my apartment and expenses up here. Because otherwise I couldn't have done it.

ME: I figured that they probably figured I fell out of touch because your sister and I had a falling-out.

HIM : Did you guys have a falling-out that was like—I don't really remember the specifics. When she has a falling-out with somebody, it's usually permanent.

M E: She felt I'd insulted her. She was talking about not knowing what to do after college. She said she wanted to teach but the job market was bad. I recommended a teaching Fulbright. She interpreted that as my saying that I thought she wasn't doing anything impressive enough. She didn't tell this to me directly. I had to learn it from a friend. When I called to apologise, explain that I hadn't meant it that way, she refused to answer my calls and never replied. So that's how that ended.

HIM : That sounds like her. Maybe she'd be happy to hear from you now.

M E: I won't reach out to her. I want to make sure I'm protecting your identity.

HIM : But when you write the book, Mark [Last Name] Ruined My Life.

M E: No, but—

HIM : Right. I'm being unkind.

M E: That's not what it's going to be. By any means. I've been thinking about this. I want to change certain identifying details so that I'm protecting your identity.

HIM : Which I appreciate.

M E: Well and then it's really weird—because I'm in the position of power. There's this weird power thing, right, which I'm very much aware of.

HIM : Yeah, you're subverting that whole dynamic.

M E: And then at the same time—if I change certain details to protect your identity, then I'm lying.

HIM : It's tough to do a deep dive on the psychology of friendship and betrayal and then change the reasons why.

M E: I don't want to—I want to be respectful of the fact that you're doing this. But I wasn't sure if your parents—they have no idea?

HIM : No, I wouldn't think.

M E: This whole thing, it's interesting. Am I saying in some way it never happened—because I didn't press charges? Pressing charges never even occurred to me. And so by not doing that, does that mean that I've provided consent? That's how I was thinking back then.

HIM : That's an unfortunate twist of logic.

M E: Fortunate for you.

HIM : Right. I mean, that works out.

DID I REALLY NEED LOCKE FOR THAT?

Two weeks have passed, and Mark still hasn't replied to my request for five good memories.

I read Locke. I'm probably simplifying here, but he said memory is a necessary condition of personal identity. So, this means Mark's personal identity—in relation to me—is my rapist.

Did I really need Locke for that?

I almost deleted the word *rapist*. But Mark used the word *rape*. I should be able to use the word *rape*. Do I really need Mark to use it before I can?

Maybe Mark chooses not to remember the good moments— because he wants the friendship never to have mattered.

Not mattering breeds indifference, or a freedom from existence.

That one night matters more than all the years of friendship. Why should I be hurt if that's his position? It's what I wanted, isn't it?

If I wrench out five fond memories from Mark, then what?

And if Mark can't come up with five good memories?

Mark said, *It's tough to do a deep dive on the psychology of friendship and betrayal and then change the reasons why.*

Can I interpret that to mean he'll approve of what I'm doing—of keeping details the same but simply neglecting any irrelevant identifying details?

Why not?

Because it'd be unethical.

I'll tell him. Eventually, I'll tell him.

...

M E: How do you think—would you have expected me to ever report it? Was that ever a concern of yours?

HIM: I mean, it was a concern of mine immediately afterward, and then I guess you didn't.

M E: Right.

HIM: But yeah, certainly you could have.

M E: It didn't occur to me.

HIM: It's helpful for me to hear your side of a lot of these things, but it's just like, I just want to give you a big hug and say I'm sorry in person.

M E: I appreciate it. And that's the thing, I genuinely appreciate it. I know I keep saying this, but I feel worried I'm going to disappoint women with this project.

HIM: You feel like you should be angrier at me.

M E: Yeah. Instead, I think back to how there were so many good times. I do wonder, if it had gone further—

HIM: Would you still have that reaction?

M E: I don't know.

HIM: I think it's probably for the best that you don't have to find out.

M E: I'm certainly mad at this other guy and at my newspaper adviser, but with you it was different. And that's why I find this interesting. In some ways, this story isn't original, and that's the story. Sexual assault happens all the time. What makes this story sort of unusual is we're having the conversation. I don't think that happens very often.

HIM : Yeah, I can't imagine.

M E: And I'm glad we're having this conversation. I told you before, when I decided to pursue this book, I thought, Oh good, I can talk to Mark. I didn't think I was allowed to talk to you before. Because of the narrative of how one is supposed to react to such events.

HIM : It really has been good to talk to you, even about this. I feel in a lot of ways the same way.

M E: That's good. I'm glad it's helpful. I'm sorry you don't really have anyone you feel like you can open up to.

HIM : Yeah, but that's more of a me problem than a you problem. It would be better if I did have someone, but it is what it is.

BUT WHAT'S IT LIKE?

I'm reading a book about metaphors. Chris asks me about it, and I try to summarise the thesis, something about how metaphors shape our perceptions and actions without our consciously realising it.

It's pretty good, I tell him.

But what's it like? he asks.

Ha, ha, I say.

I'm now considering my figurative language surrounding the assault:

I became rigid, like an animal who senses it's impossible to bolt.

I cried, quietly, as if in public.

In the first instance, I'm not human. In the second, Mark is a stranger.

I stare at the ceiling fan and wonder: why store our friendship forever in that basement?

The basement is a metaphor. The perfect metaphor. The Freudian metaphor. The id lives in the basement, right?

This impulse to find metaphors, it's because I want to describe feelings that don't have words. Or maybe there is a word for this—for missing the friend who sexually assaulted you. The German language has a word for everything, it seems like. Is there a word for the fear of hearing one's own voice?

And does Mark not understand that saying he wants to hug me is actually pretty creepy? And yet, after his hug comment, I said, *I appreciate it.* And I then apologised for his not having anyone else he can confide in. I think Leigh-Anne would title this project, *An Obvious Performance of Gender.*

I need to power through the transcription.

...

ME: Self-absorbed question: was it obvious in high school that I was having psychiatric problems?

HIM: I remember you being—no, I don't recall you being sad. You at least at the surface level were, you had all that energy. You were so earnest about everything, it seemed like. It was really endearing. But no, I wouldn't say you came off as damaged or disturbed.

ME: I guess it's easier to see when somebody is depressed, but when they're hypomanic or manic—

HIM: Yeah, I guess the mania—I was aware you were having manic episodes, but at the time I didn't realise what that implied. In high school you were just this super-achiever. I remember you wanting me to try so much harder.

ME: I remember Daniel's mom asking me to take Daniel with me to college. She said I made him work. I remember wanting everybody to work harder. I guess I probably was pretty earnest. I guess it's good—I never felt like anything came easily to me. Which is probably why I work so hard.

HIM: Whether or not it comes easily, it does seem to come to you.

ME: I never know how to stop working. The idea of a vacation never occurs to me. When I think of leaving the house, I think of going to a café to do work. Or going to a bookstore or a library for more books.

HIM : It's funny because my own experience is different in that way. I never had to try. Physics was the first class where I couldn't just hear what the teacher said once and know it. I feel like I was going somewhere more interesting than that, than just saying I was smart in high school. I guess what I'm saying is I had been told I was really smart my entire life and I resented the expectations that were on me.

M E: That's why psychologists tell parents not to tell their kids that they're so smart or so talented. Parents are supposed to compliment the action. That way, when the kid does poorly, she won't see it as a reflection of her core self.

HIM : I remember: I think I was in college when I realised I'm pretty smart, but I'm not that smart. I'm not going to be the next Einstein or the next Feynman or the next name-your-physicist-here. I'm just a guy.

M E: Was that hard for you then, in college? Do you think that also led to dropping out? Realising that it wasn't going to come naturally and then it was some reflection of your core self?

HIM : I mean, did I have a hard time reconceptualising myself as a not-genius? Yeah, that took some processing. But I dropped out more because I was having crippling anxiety attacks. Which I don't really think were necessarily related to that.

M E: I think a lot of people would think of a genius as needing to work hard. So I don't think it's any indication of your intelligence that physics didn't always come easily.

HIM : Right. Einstein is a good example of this. He was preternaturally gifted, but he wanted to do physics enough that he wanted to do physics in his spare time. He wrote four epoch-changing papers in the course of one year when he was twenty-something. Twenty-three or something like that. I'm not that guy.

ME: Certainly, leaving high school, going to college, being in a new setting, and realising, Oh my gosh, there's so much I don't know.

HIM: And I think everybody goes through that. I have a bad habit of rationalising my tortured genius, I feel like. Which I don't want to do. I don't find that narrative all that interesting.

ME: What do you think is most interesting about this project? If it's possible for you to remove yourself and imagine it from an outsider's perspective.

HIM: I can understand why you would want to write about it. Because it is an unusual situation to find yourself in. Because I feel like most rape victims are not close to the people that rape them. Or don't remain close, anyway. It's been interesting, it's been good, to hear your side of things. I feel like you have very different reactions to what happened than I would have expected, or than people generally would have expected. So that's interesting. To see what your thoughts on what happened are. That's kind of a dumb answer.

ME: No, that's really helpful for me to know. To turn this around, do you have questions for me? Is there something you've wanted to ask me?

HIM: Did you feel like you needed to forgive me?

ME: No. I don't think I ever felt like I needed to forgive you. I've wondered about that. Like, Why am I not angrier? I'm supposed to be angry. And I don't—

HIM: You had to have felt, just—

ME: I was hurt, and sort of surprised. My dad's death complicates it. Because honestly, I remember when stuff happened with my newspaper adviser, I didn't want my dad to know. Which is why I didn't want to tell my mom. I eventually did tell my mom. She told my dad. And when he found out, I was devastated because I knew how much he hated—he couldn't—a father—

HIM : Sure, he would have wanted to protect you.

M E: Right. So after what happened between us, in some messed-up way, I remember feeling relief that I didn't have to keep this from my dad, and he wouldn't have to feel bad, and therefore I didn't—again, the patriarchy, literally patriarchy.

HIM : Your own emotions are contingent on protecting your father's.

M E: Yes. And I just was so—I was also, I don't remember, I honestly don't remember feeling angry, and this could be—and this is the whole danger of this project. Just as a therapist may think she knows more about the patient than the patient knows, the reader, I'm realising—and I'll probably put this in the book verbatim, but I'm realising that the reader, I am running the risk of the reader thinking or feeling that she knows more about me than I know, in terms of my reaction. If put into the context of a sociology textbook—

HIM : If you're writing about your fifteen years of rethinking it, versus your immediate reaction at the time—

M E: Right. But I do remember my immediate reaction. I don't think I was lying when I told you back then, I forgive you, just read *Franny and Zooey*. I didn't feel angry at you. I felt angry at my newspaper adviser. I felt angry at the friend who raped me years later. I don't talk to him anymore, and I would never reach back out to him.

HIM : I wouldn't imagine.

M E: But with you, we had this history, and I felt conflicted, because I felt you were a good person who did something bad. But also, I think my first boyfriend—there was such an age difference. I was a high school freshman and he was a high school senior. He got me to do a lot of things that I didn't want to do. And so I think I was associating anything sexual with—

HIM : Right. This is just what guys do.

M E: And it's up to what the men want.

HIM : That's a shame.

M E: I know so many women who've been sexually assaulted. It's just so common. I think I also thought, It could have been worse. I don't know why I can't feel angry.

HIM : Do you think you weren't allowing yourself to feel angry? I don't want to push you on this. I feel gross—

M E: No, there's been enough distance. I'm asking you to ask me. I'm writing about this.

HIM : There's a part of me that knows that, and the part of me that just—it just still feels, I don't know, unseemly to—this is just maybe my Midwestern prudishness.

THE THINGS YOU'RE SUPPOSED TO DO

I told him: *But I do remember my immediate reaction—I don't think I was lying when I told you back then, I forgive you.* That's not right. My immediate reaction, which I still can't remember, is one he remembers: I cried and whispered, he raped me.

I'm behind on grading and still need to file my taxes.

I call Nina, ask her, Do you ever not do the things you're supposed to do—even though you know you should do them and that if you did do them you'd feel happier?

She laughs, offers an emphatic yes.

I just described procrastination, didn't I? I ask.

Yes, she says. Everybody does that.

I confide in a colleague, My students submitted essays three weeks ago, and I still haven't returned grades.

I haven't returned papers that students gave me at the start of the semester, she says.

So I won't be fired? I ask.

Do you realise how hard it'd be to get fired?

I almost, finally, file my taxes. But before clicking submit, I am offered *protection* in the event I'm audited. TurboTax is what, a gruff Italian mobster? I then spend five hours researching the likelihood I'll be audited. I sort of eyeballed my deductions. I mean, nobody actually goes receipt by receipt. Right? Mark used to work at a tax place.

201

But no, I will not ask him to make amends by reviewing my taxes. That'd be absurd. Though the fact that I'm even interviewing him is absurd. But no, I won't ask him to review my taxes.

...

M E: I think also this was the other key piece. It'd been a year since my dad died. And just my whole life, everything, I was so devoted to him. Any time anything bad happened after he died, I just thought, Well, the worst thing has already happened. Nothing will be as bad as that. And therefore, I decided, I'm not going to spend time thinking about anything else bad—

HIM : That makes a kind of sense.

M E: I think it makes sense that this is what I want to write about after writing the book for my dad. When I think about that being out of the way—

HIM : If you already wrote about the most important thing, now you have the space to write about what else happened.

M E: And it's just now—last week, I was giving a reading, reading from my book, and suddenly I realised, I'm missing my dad. I'd read from the book so many times. But suddenly, in reading it this time, I felt—I remembered: he's really gone. Though I'm not obsessing about him anymore. Probably because of the book, medication, whatever. He doesn't obsess me.

HIM : That's good.

M E: I think one reason this project interests me—after the election, I thought about what happened between us a lot. I also thought a lot about my newspaper adviser and this other guy.

HIM : Having a sexual predator as president, I see how that could bring that on.

M E: I was just so—I was having nightmares a lot. I got mad at this history professor where I work. He said something like, At least with our side, real change will start to happen. I told him that in the moment, it's hard to see things that way. I told him that women—among so many other groups—are having a hard time processing—because we now have a president, on record, bragging about sexually assaulting women. And the history prof said to me that I'd made an inappropriate comment. I thought, Because I acknowledged that sexual assault exists, that's inappropriate? But I didn't tell him that. I felt too angry to speak.

HIM : That's a strange reaction—on his part.

M E: Trump insulted basically every group. It's not just women. But I think it was seeing the video come out, and Republicans still getting behind him even though he's on tape—

HIM : It's depressing.

M E: And then the way they talked about women: It could have been my daughter or my wife or my mother or my sister. It's like, you don't have to connect this to women in relation to you. A woman can be a woman.

HIM : Right, but I feel like that's how a lot of guys process—that's the only way they're able to relate to women's issues. By the context of paternalism. Not super productive.

M E: So when I thought to write about this, I did wonder if it'd stop the nightmares. And I can take the story from a relatively new angle. I mean, I'm sure someone has done this. But it hasn't been done that much.

HIM : I haven't seen too many sympathetic portraits of, you know, my own rapist.

M E: Is it weird for you—the definition?

HIM : I had never really thought about it, associated it with that word, but if that's the definition, then it is what it is. I don't like that that word applies to me. But I guess it does.

M E: I'm interested in examining the complexity of all this.

HIM : And if you're going to write it, you may as well really do the job. Obviously, it's uncomfortable for me to be the subject, but that's fine.

M E: I'm glad we're talking again. If there's anything—if there's any way to make it up to me, this is definitely it.

HIM : Well, I'm glad I can do that for you.

M E: I should let you go. We've been talking for a while now.

HIM : Like I was saying, I don't have a huge amount of plans. I don't know if it's neither here nor there, but when we were close, I was not doing photography. I will email you—I went out immediately after our last conversation, or the next day, I took some photos I like. I don't know, at least in context. I don't know if they have some sort of—I'd just be curious to see what you think.

M E: I'd love to see them.

HIM : I work for a camera shop, so over the years I've picked up a few things. I'm not a photographer of any great note.

M E: Have you thought about doing professional photography for a magazine or newspaper or—

HIM : To really control a portrait session, you need to have a little bit more of an extroverted personality than I do. I do some product photos at work for our website. Which is fine, but it's not all that exciting. I do more urbex-y sort of stuff on my own time. You should have just gotten an email with a link. You don't have to look right now. It's fine. Just because it was like—they were in some way a reaction to that conversation.

M E: These are really great.

HIM : Oh, well. Thank you.

M E: Oh, wow. Thanks for the metaphors.

HIM : Well, that's why I figured it might be useful to you.

M E: These are amazing.

HIM : It's nice of you to say. It's an abandoned factory maybe five or ten minutes from where I work.

M E: This is so thoughtful. Really, thank you.

HIM : You're welcome. As best I can figure, it was some sort of power station. It was right next to a railway. It's in obvious ruin, which is fun.

M E: The contrast—

HIM : Yeah, I was going for a really high contrast.

M E: And I like the focal point. In this one with the tyre. I like how the focal point is on the stairs—

HIM : Just go metaphor crazy. It's fine.

M E: And near the stairs—

HIM : Yeah, there's a big pile of collapsed ceiling.

M E: Basically, I like where you have the focal point.

HOW DOES THIS ALL END?

I share both transcripts with Jung and Molly. We meet at the same restaurant where we met before. I make sure there are no children sitting near us this time.

I find it annoying that he went out and took photos, Molly says.

Oh. I thought that was really nice of him, I say.

Jung looks at me, like: huh?

I mean, he's in a tough rhetorical position, I reply.

Jung and Molly look down at the table. They seem unsure of how to talk about this.

It's OK, I tell them. I sent you the transcripts because I genuinely want your criticisms.

If the rape is all he remembers of you, Jung asks, then what does that say about your friendship?

Maybe it mattered so much, I say, that the good memories now feel painful to him.

Jung eyes my eyes. I think of Aristotle's belief that friends provide us with self-knowledge that might otherwise be hard to grasp. We deceive ourselves of our motives, even when we don't mean to.

I know, I tell her, I know. I'm defending him.

How do you feel? Molly asks.

Confused, I answer.

I'm curious, Jung says, about where you both end up. How does this all end?

Oh, I intend to cut off communication with Mark when this is done.

That's so interesting, Molly says. I hadn't considered.

I just realised that, I said. I hadn't really thought about where this would all end. I guess because I don't see Mark and me keeping in touch. Is that bad?

No, Molly says. It makes sense.

It's not me ending the friendship, right? He ended it.

I wouldn't feel bad, Jung says. I think it's strange that he can't come up with five good memories.

Now I'm really wondering, *What was this friendship?* I feel stupid for having defended him to Jung and Molly. Sure, I came up with a lot of memories, I told them, but I'm a memoirist. It's what I do.

But really: how can he not recall five specific memories?

Reminiscing about our friendship suddenly seems like the sun casting a fake specialness on a pile of trash. But I want to find the nice memories that were thrown away.

I return to the audio. I listen to Mark say, *It was a huge betrayal.*

His voice: assertive, reflexive, matter-of-fact.

His voice, as I remember it when he apologised: hesitant, rickety.

I meet with Adam.

I don't think my friends believe me, I tell him, when I say that I'm not angry.

Others' disbelief, Adam says, that's its own topic.

But what if I don't know how I feel? Am I wrong? Is this like when therapists think they know more about their patients than their patients know about themselves?

A real therapist is not going to think that, Adam explains. Maybe sidewalk psychology says that. The point of modern therapy is to say anything and to feel anything.

I feel hurt, I tell Adam, that Mark hasn't sent me five good memories.

Not that I would hope one way or the other, Adam says, but it could be just as good, sort of grist for the mill, if he's not able to. So much to write about there. I'm almost hoping he doesn't. It's just another layer. Also, I don't know if your books about anger touch on this, but I have found that underneath anger are usually two things at work: guilt or fear. Sometimes it's both. But one of those is always there. Sometimes you have to dig deep to identify the fear, but it could be anything and it's usually about us. It's usually about ourselves. There's something we're afraid of. It could have to do with emotional security or financial security. But underneath the anger is usually some degree of fear or guilt.

That makes sense, I tell him. We feel many things at once. Feelings within other feelings.

PART FOUR:
THE VISIT

I REALISE MY HANDS ARE SHAKING

Five weeks after I requested them, Mark sends, finally, five good memories:

> Making it through my morning classes to lunch and sitting across a table from you and talking about everything and nothing for 15–20 minutes, and maybe teasing Garrett for having watched Office Space yet again the night before.

> Tagging along with friends to go to Steak & Shake while you were working, and eating cheese fries and frisco melts and laughing and talking with you for five minutes between tables and leaving what seemed like extravagant tips for a high schooler with a part-time job.

> I visited you at Northwestern and we rode the L into Belmont and spent an afternoon browsing through record stores and weird little boutiques, and then I dragged you downtown to go to the observation deck at the Sears Tower only I had us walk a mile in the wrong direction to the John Hancock building which was closed (sorry!).

> In the summer after our freshman year in college, Carlos and I somehow talked you into coming to a sportscar race at Mid-Ohio, and we sat on the bleachers in the sun and watched cars go by.

I also remember staying up too late watching weird movies in the little room at the top of the stairs in your parents' house, and monopolising that giant papasan chair you had whenever I could.

Until now, I forgot the third memory. And I feel such relief: he possesses a memory that I can't reconstruct. This seems like proof that he valued our friendship. But if he valued it, then why did he ruin it?

In his email, he explained why it took him so long to send the memories:

I really didn't intend to ignore this for so long, but I sort of got knocked off my equilibrium, and I guess I needed some time to build up a little bit of mental distance from all this again (is that awful of me?). I suppose I'm also a bit embarrassed at how sparse my own memories—good and bad—of those years have become. I've had a frustrating amount of difficulty in recalling specific moments, as opposed to general impressions.

I reply to Mark, thanking him for the five good memories, and we arrange to see one another in June.

I sit at my computer to buy a round-trip plane ticket to visit him, but instead buy tickets for a movie showing around the corner.

I just need to get out of my head, I tell Chris.

The synopsis: a woman unwittingly commits herself to a psychiatric facility where her stalker becomes a staffer. I should have researched this before buying tickets.

Chris whispers, Do you want to leave?

I almost ask why, but I realise my hands are shaking.

No, I'm fine, I whisper back.

After the film ends, I tell Chris, The stalker, he looked like Mark. The facial hair and glasses. It was unnerving.

I call Sarah, describe the movie where the actor resembled Mark.

If I can't watch a movie where an actor resembles Mark, I tell her, how am I going to visit him?

You don't have to visit him, she says. Honestly, I don't care about his take.

Really?

I don't, she says. His voice, his excuses, none of that interests me.

But then the reader is left with what? I ask her. My interior life?

We laugh.

I like the way you're thinking, I say, but I could use more scenes for the book. Though I don't know if I can really see him.

So don't, she says. You don't have to see him. I care about your reflection.

I ask my editor what she thinks.

It's up to you, she says. Putting concerns about the book aside, I think seeing him would be good. It might provide closure. There's something about speaking in person that's different from speaking on the phone.

IS THAT THE RIGHT WAY TO LIVE?

Ever since Adam mentioned that I have grandiose tendencies, I've been second-guessing my intentions.

Do you think there's something grandiose to writing? I ask Adam. To think: *complete strangers will read this because I have something to say*.

To some degree, Adam says, there has to be something in you where you feel worth it. Where is that typically? Hundreds of thousands of people have already done this. To not write a book at that point might feel like low self-worth, or lack of confidence. Instead of a writer, think of a doctor or a therapist. Does that mean that a doctor or therapist is grandiose because they think they can help somebody? They're meddling in other people's affairs. Or a cop: *I think I'm the right guy who can supervise everybody in my town*. But if we were Laverne and Shirley at the walk-in brewery, putting caps on bottles, is that the right way to live if we felt like we had something different to give the world?

That makes me feel better, I tell him.

And why do I believe this project is worth it? Because so many perpetrators of sexual assault are regular guys, and I want to show that. I also want to show how I made—back then and even very recently—excuses for Mark, even though I know better. I really thought I'd handle my interviews with Mark differently. I thought I'd interrogate him. So much for my *If He Says No/Yes* boasting.

HE USED HIS FINGERS TO RAPE HIS VICTIM

Mark and I email back and forth, trying to figure out when and where to meet. My emails to him are crafted without seeming crafted. I am going for casual. I don't want any more overwrought messages about *the most impregnable emotional barriers* and *desperate self-preservation*. I want to reach him, not the guy trying to say all the right things.

I ask him to recommend quiet restaurants or cafés, and in his email reply he writes, *I feel like there's a definite shortage of listicles offering to tell me what the 15 best places for this would be.*

I laugh and feel uncomfortable about laughing. I want to access anger. I should move the emails into a business-casual direction. But what's the tonal equivalent of black slacks and a nice blouse?

I watch a movie about a woman who realises, decades later, that she was raped as a teenager—and it scares me, this premise. She blocked the rapist's actions. But I never really blocked Mark's. All along I could say that he carried me into his basement room, undressed me, put his fingers in my vagina, and told me to be quiet. I just can't bring myself to acknowledge that his actions fit the definition of rape.

I tell Chris, I still have trouble labelling it, what Mark did to me, rape.

Chris asks, Are there different degrees of rape?

It differs by state, I tell him. There are all these confusing overlapping codes because laws keep getting revised. And a lot of states don't even use the term *rape*.

Have you looked into that Brock Turner case? Chris asks. I think he used an object to rape his victim.

He used his fingers.

In January of 2015, Brock Turner used his fingers to rape his unconscious victim, referred to as Emily Doe, on the ground behind a dumpster. The judge sentenced Turner to only six months in county jail. Turner served three. Politicians, media outlets, and his victim referred to him as a rapist. But in California, at that time, using one's fingers to penetrate a victim was a less serious sexual offence. More than a year later, in response to public outcry about the case, the California State Legislature unanimously passed two bills: one bill would update California's legal definition of rape to cover digital penetration, and the other bill would provide a mandatory minimum three-year prison sentence for the sexual assault of an intoxicated or unconscious person. The governor signed them into law in September of 2016.

And this, I realise, is why using the word *rape* matters. Because Emily Doe used the word *rape*, I now feel comfortable using it too. And if I can use the word *rape* to describe Mark's actions, maybe some readers of this book—who also have been raped in the same way—won't diminish what happened to them.

Mark raped me.

UNDERWATER

Classes end, and I submit grades—and I just want to relax. But it's almost June, and I still haven't bought the plane tickets to visit Mark.

I ask Chris if he'll help me book the trip.

Sure, what do you need help with? he asks.

I just want you to stand near me while I handle it. That's all.

Chris watches me pick flights and type my credit card number.

Isn't this fun? I ask him.

I load the Airbnb site, and Chris says, Why don't you stay at a hotel?

Because in my funding proposal to the English Department, I said I'd use Airbnb. Though I really don't want to deal with plug-in air fresheners and a bad mattress.

Stay at a hotel, Chris says. You'll be able to relax more easily.

There's a chance I won't get reimbursed, I tell him.

But I take Chris's advice, splurging on a room at the Hilton.

Now I really feel anxious about seeing Mark. I swim laps, thinking that might relax me. But each time I go underwater, flashbacks of the rape come at me. Only one other swimmer is in the pool, and he's several lanes away. The next time I go underwater, I scream—and it feels good. And nobody heard. I didn't want anybody to, of course. I wonder if any gender studies academics have explored reclusive screaming. I should ask Leigh-Anne.

BRAVE?

I'm on an Amtrak train to New York. I'm supposed to give a reading there tonight, but really I'm using it as an excuse to see friends. Nina insisted I stay the night with her. And Sarah told me she wanted to discuss my project because she knows I'm seeing Mark later this week.

Across the aisle, a man and a woman, both in suits, share a laptop. She tells him that she feels guilty for not doing more. He tells her how useful she's been to the team.

I just don't want the others to think I'm not pulling my weight, she says.

This fear, so many women have it: *I'm not doing enough. I should be doing more.*

Jung texts me while I'm on the train, asks if I've booked my trip to visit Mark. I reply that I leave in four days. *You're the bravest person I know right now*, she texts back.

Brave? I hadn't considered this brave. I don't feel brave.

I'm nervous.

But I remind myself that Mark probably feels way more nervous.

At the bookstore, an hour before the event, I consider reading from this project, but decide that could be upsetting for anybody in the audience who's been raped. So I read from the beginning of my first book. I likely could recite it from memory by now.

Afterward, I head to Nina's apartment, and she tells me how helpful this project has been to her.

Ever since you started working on it, she says, it's gotten me thinking more about my ex. That's a good thing. I'm confronting the rape. I've really been thinking about how manipulative he was. He listed all the ways he was going to ruin me. First, he said he'd send this sex tape to my master's programme. He said he'd send it to my internship boss. And I was like, Fine, go ahead. Send them the video. I don't care. But then he threatened to send it to my parents, and I freaked out. He knew they were my weakness. Having their view of me stay intact, that was important. I told him he couldn't send it to them. Then he pushed the threat harder, said if I didn't have sex with him again, he'd send the tape to my parents. I think he recognised the cultural difference. He was white, and he knew I came from a traditional Indian household. And I never wanted to tape us having sex. That was all for him.

How much older was he? I ask her.

Seven years older, she says, and I figured, *OK, this is what adults do in a relationship.* I was still in undergrad, and I wanted to seem more adult. So when he threatened to send them the tape, I agreed to sleep with him again. There was no point where I said, Stop.

How are you feeling about it?

I feel like I'm still in the process of understanding my feelings, she says. How about you?

Same, I tell her. Would it offend you if I used the word rape when describing what Mark did?

Nina laughs.

No, she says. Of course not.

Are you sure?

Yes, I'm sure. Oh my gosh. Of course it wouldn't offend me.

And then we're both laughing.

Before I catch my train back to Baltimore, Sarah and I meet for coffee near Penn Station.

When do you visit Mark? she asks.

At the end of this week, I tell her, and I don't know how to greet him. I mean, it'd be too weird to hug him. A handshake is too professional.

It's like you're about to climb Mount Everest, she says, but you're worried about stepping on a bug before you get on the mountain.

WE HAVE TO KEEP MAKING ART

Rebekah calls me when I'm at the Baltimore airport.

When do you leave to see Mark? she asks.

In an hour, I say. I'm meeting up with him tomorrow evening.

That's this weekend? she says. How are you feeling?

Nervous, I tell her. But mostly because I don't know what else I can really get out of him. He's answered most of my questions.

TV screens are showing the latest news story: families seeking asylum in the United States are being separated at the border.

It's hard to focus on this project, I tell Rebekah, when our country is committing blatant human rights violations.

I understand why you're feeling that way, she says. But please don't stop working on this project. We have to keep making art. If we stop, then the other side wins.

I tell her about my friend Tom's project, the one he's doing about ISIS.

I probably shouldn't say ISIS at an airport, I whisper, and then I worry that by whispering, I'm actually drawing even more attention to myself. Oh, and I should get going. It looks like my flight is boarding.

In line for boarding, the man in front of me asks, So what's bringing you to Ohio?

Work, I say.

He's pale-skinned, thin, looks fortyish but has a kid's face—freckles dabbing his small nose and big cheeks. He wears a blue polo shirt tucked into dark jeans with a braided belt.

What's your work? he asks.

Writing, I tell him.

Maybe I'll sit next to you on the flight? I'd love to hear more about your writing.

I think, *No you wouldn't*. Unfortunately, this airline doesn't do assigned seating.

Once inside the plane, I search for a middle seat and apologise to the women on either side.

The flight attendant said it's a full flight, I explain.

Sit, sit, they say—almost in unison.

We retire to our antisocial airplane props: magazine, movie, book, headphones. I open my notebook, tell myself, *Write about your feelings*. Instead, I write about booking, when I was twenty-three, a one-way ticket, New York to Paris, to declare my love for a man twice my age. He was a screenwriter. I'd met him at a magazine party in New York. But he lived in London, not Paris. My rationale: *if I'm already on his side of the Atlantic, I can drop in casually*. I explained this to French border control agents suspicious of my one-way ticket. I told them that I wanted to seem less desperate to the man. I told them that I'd be staying in Paris with another man, a French citizen. The man I was travelling for, I told them, he was an American screenwriter working in London. He divided his time between there and New York.

What's his name? the agents wanted to know.

Which one? I asked.

The French one.

Cyril, I said.

Cyril what? they asked.

Cyril taught literature at a university in Paris, or maybe right outside Paris. He belonged to something called the Jockey

Club (Proust mentions it, he'd elaborated, in *À la recherche du temps perdu*). He published political satire under a pseudonym in obscure French literary magazines. I knew that much. But Cyril's last name escaped me. Or maybe he never mentioned it. We'd met six months prior, in a Manhattan bookstore. I'd been reading Apollinaire when he introduced himself. We then spent the weekend together, meandering through the city and discussing books, before he returned to Paris. Come with me, he'd said, but I was already infatuated with the screenwriter (who seemed completely unaware of my feelings, though we emailed almost every day). In the months since then, Cyril and I had emailed. His email address translated to count of the dispossessed, or something like that, in Basque or another dying language. But I didn't learn that until months after corresponding with him. By then I felt too embarrassed to ask him his last name; it seemed like something I should know.

You don't know his last name? one agent asked.

No one travels like this, the other agent said.

So I told them, You're just jealous because I'm twenty-three and unencumbered.

And that's when they left me alone in a small room.

I genuinely didn't see the problem. I wasn't transporting cocaine or firearms. And who wouldn't book a transatlantic flight that cost less than $300?

When the agents returned, they searched my bags—heavy with poetry books—and laughed while reading my journals.

What's so funny? I asked.

They laughed harder.

I knew they were judging my sappy entries about the screenwriter. Yet things could have been worse. I deserved worse. But I was a young, well-dressed white American woman. My only repercussions? The agents stamped my passport with a travel deadline. I had one month in France, which was fine by me. It gave structure to my otherwise disorganised trip.

And why am I thinking about that trip? I'm not exactly sure. It was such a stupid, probably manic thing to do: flying across the ocean to stay in Paris with somebody whose last name I didn't know—only because I wanted to drop into London to declare my love to some other acquaintance. And I did declare my love to the screenwriter. Over drinks at a London pub, I confided that I'd actually made the trip to tell him my feelings. And he told me he had a girlfriend. But then he invited me back to the house he shared with her, said she wouldn't be home for a few hours, and I had sex with him there. I never thought I would do something like that, but I did. And for the next two years, whenever he visited New York, I'd sleep with him.

The plane lands, and I take a cab to the hotel. I am so glad I followed Chris's advice. The hotel has a bar, a nice restaurant, a gym, a pool. I sit by the big window in my room, open my notebook, and think about my first paying job: motel maid. My first week there, a man invited me into his room. I was thirteen years old. He must have been at least fifty, though at thirteen it's hard to guess adults' general ages. I told him I had to work, and he told me he wouldn't tell. I slipped into the nearest room and locked the door. He knocked, said, I won't tell. I called the main desk, said that the man in whatever room he was in needed assistance. Strange that I'm only now remembering this. Or: not at all strange.

I'm reconstructing scenes from the past—when I should be reflecting on my feelings about *now*.

I write *I feel* and then draw a blank—as in, a line for a blank. I do this down the page.

I feel _____

I feel _____

I feel _____

I feel _____

I feel _____

I feel _____

I feel _____

I feel _____

I find the hotel bar.

The bartender asks me what I'll have, and I tell him a cocktail probably. But I need a moment.

Do you want something sweet or dry?

I like vodka-based cocktails, I say. I just need a minute to decide.

I'm going to make you a Pretty in Pink, he says and disappears before I can object.

I open my notebook, tell myself, *Reflect on the rape.* I write: *I know how to order a drink.*

Sports games play on the two absurdly large flat-screen TVs above the bar—except the third screen shows MSNBC. The journalists are covering the child migrants. I'm reading the subtitles—*These are prisons. We're jailing babies*—when the channel suddenly changes to sports.

Hey, the other bartender says. I was watching that.

The remote is in my bartender's hand. My bartender disgusts me, or I am transferring my disgust for the current administration to my bartender.

He returns with some magenta-looking liquid, and I stupidly thank him. I try it, and he doesn't even ask if I like it. I don't. I should tell him. But I don't.

I write: *I didn't want Pretty in Pink, and now I'm going to pay twelve dollars for this disgusting cocktail.*

The man next to me asks what I'm working on.

Work, I say.

He looks at me, expecting more.

I'm under a deadline, I say.

I get it, he says. You don't want to talk to me.

It's a tight deadline, I explain.

It must be. You'd be crazy to do work at a bar.

I smile a closed-lips smile. Why do I smile?

You from the area? he asks.

Baltimore, I tell him.

What brings you here then?

I'm here to interview the guy who raped me fourteen years ago. But I don't say that.

Work, I answer.

I ask the bartender for the check, and he looks at my glass. Did you not like the cocktail?

No, I tell him. It's too sweet.

He doesn't charge me for it, and I thank him. Why thank him for not charging me for what I did not order? Yet I do, twice: Really, thank you.

Back in my hotel room, I review my manuscript, consider the holes. I really need to reflect on how the rape altered my perception of myself.

I doubt it did. If anything, it cemented my sense of self. I already knew I cared too much about a man's comfort. About a man's approval. How many times did I tell men, in my twenties, after they rolled over in bed, That was amazing—a complete lie.

And that screenwriter, I'm now remembering, he refused to use condoms, and so after we'd have sex, he'd give me cash for the morning-after pill. And I genuinely considered him sweet and responsible. He always gave me the exact amount.

That way you don't feel like a prostitute, he said.

This is uncomfortable. I need to move around. Endorphins will help me think.

I change into shorts, sneakers, and a T-shirt. Only one other guest is at the hotel gym. I'm happy the guest is a woman, because now I can experiment with these weight machines without feeling self-conscious. I hate reading the directions when men are nearby. A broad-shouldered man almost always intervenes, explaining how the machine works, what to do, what muscles the machine will work, and so on. And the man usually tells me, Start small. But today, with no men around, I confidently move from machine to machine. Turns out they are fairly self-explanatory.

I shower, put on pyjamas, get ready for bed, open my notebook.

I feel _____

I feel _____

I feel _____

I feel _____

I feel _____

I feel _____

I feel _____

I feel _____

Mark signed his initial email *Your friend*—probably because I'd led him to believe that we were becoming friends again.

I close my notebook and play a history podcast. The hosts are talking about upside-down crucifixion. I turn off the lights.

NOT MUCH SOUND TRAVELS HERE

Today I see Mark. We agreed to meet at the local art museum. I'm wearing what I'd otherwise wear—dark fitted jeans, pink tie-front blouse, brown summer oxfords—after deciding that I should wear what I would have worn had I not been thinking about what to wear.

I considered a white tie-front blouse but decided on the pink. Pink might throw him off, make me seem sweet as opposed to manipulative.

Or: he will sense that I'm wearing pink so as to catch him off guard.

Or: he will not even think about my outfit because he now is a progressive man who regrets his past and will be cautious about looking at me anywhere but in my eyes.

Likely: the outfit is irrelevant.

If he's wearing anything moderately professional, how do I interpret that?

Questions. What are my questions? So far, these are all I have:

Where did/do you see this relationship going?

How have you been feeling since we last spoke?

How would you feel if your parents found out? What would you tell them?

Have you had crushes on women since the ~~assault~~ rape?

What about this project scares you the most?

Have you been running anything in your head since we last spoke?

Is this giving you closure?

Are you going to read the book?

These are not enough. But I want to riff off his answers. And I don't want to be too prepared. Just prepared enough. Articulate and casual, serious but moderately nonchalant.

I call Leigh-Anne and ask, When you, as a sociologist, interview subjects, what's your approach?

I think of a central question, she says, or one narrative or idea that I'm trying to answer. Then I think of how to get there with indirect questions.

One of my big questions, I tell her, is why did he and Jake carry me into that basement?

I don't so much know if he'll ever admit to that, she says. Because that would mean it was premeditated, and I don't think he can get himself there. I'm not saying he was plotting it for months. The point is, he always had the propensity to do it. Mark knew, the moment he decided to carry you from upstairs, a safe space, and into the basement, his space, that he would commit the act. That's the reckoning that he's doing right now. He may have thought of himself as the nice guy. And Jake could have convinced himself that Mark was a nice guy. But Jake also knew that Mark had the propensity to commit the act.

So Mark probably won't fess up to that, I say.

I highly doubt it, she says. But you can try to lead him there.

What interests you, as an academic, about this project?

I'm interested in how masculinity impacted his perception of self, she says. You might ask him: What did or does it mean, to him, to be a man? What messages did he get that made him think this would be OK? How did this influence how he sees himself as a man? And I'm interested in how masculinity is reproduced in masculine relationships.

He was living with Jake and Jake's uncle, I tell her. I remember issues of *Playboy* and *Maxim* all over the place. I remember how Jake's uncle would rate women on a scale of one to ten. Mark said that Jake's uncle was a pig. That environment had to have affected him.

Definitely, she says. You could ask him more about that. And if he gives you an answer you don't really agree with, you may need to play along—just to get further. Remember: he'll be looking at your body language.

I'm interested in why he viewed himself as a nice guy, I tell her. Did he see himself as sensitive, trustworthy, and decent? Or was it all a manipulation tactic?

You might ask him what one of the bad guys looked like. Guys from your high school.

That's good. You're really good. I miss you.

I jot Leigh-Anne's advice on some loose-leaf paper and slip it into my binder. I grab my tote bag and purse. The tote bag, perfect: it's from the independent feminist bookstore in Chicago. If I get stressed, I can look at it and think about Rebekah. I get into the hallway and realise I should check my make-up. Did I remember mascara? My God, what does mascara matter? But it does. I'll feel confident with mascara. I remember when the psych ward nurses refused to allow me eyeliner and mascara, so I used a crayon from the activities table, even though I knew it was probably covered with germs. I knew it might cause some eye infection, like that time the sample pencil eyeliner in a Sephora left my eyes irritated for a week. But without defined eyes, I look haggard. I return to my room, and yes, I'm wearing (allegedly waterproof) mascara. I request the Lyft. I get to the elevator and realise I forgot an umbrella. It might rain. And then I'll feel uncomfortable. And this blouse, it's too thin to tolerate heavy rain. But the Lyft driver is only three minutes away. Do I have time? I check my weather app. Eighty percent chance of rain within the next hour. The driver will leave after four minutes upon arrival if I am not there. But the umbrella. I run back to my room, grab the umbrella, run to the elevator. But it's full, and a bunch of the floor buttons are pushed. Monsters, these guests.

I make it outside just as the Lyft driver pulls up.

He asks where I'm from, and I say Baltimore.

Beautiful city, he says. You have a nice waterfront. No basketball, though.

No. And that's the only sport I like to watch. And thanks to my partner, I sort of glean the obscure inner workings of the NBA. And he's into NBA gossip as if it's a soap opera. Did one of LeBron's teammates really date LeBron's mom? I've heard it might not be true.

Delonte West. Yeah. That's the rumour.

And then LeBron went to Miami, which sort of fuelled the rumour.

That's an interesting situation, actually. West has bipolar disorder. That probably had a lot to do with it.

I didn't know that

Yeah, he came forward about his bipolar, and the media tore him apart. I dated a woman, for several years, with bipolar disorder, and I saw how hard that was on her. And I used to be one of these guys who didn't believe in mental illness. I didn't consider it a serious issue. But I see it a lot differently now.

A lot of NBA players are discussing their mental health, I say. I appreciate that these men—who are in a field where masculinity is valorised—are making themselves vulnerable.

Absolutely, he says. People have got to get help. There's no shame in it. Bipolar is a serious illness. The woman I dated, I don't blame her for how she treated me. Friends of mine can't understand why I'm not angry. But she couldn't help so much of her behaviour. I saw her struggling with meds. It's a bad illness.

How do you explain your lack of anger to your friends? I ask.

I don't think they'll ever understand it, he says. I stopped trying to explain it.

Even though Mark and I agreed to meet in the museum's lounge, I find a seat in the restaurant. I explain that I need to interview someone, and the server seats me in the corner.

Not much sound travels here, she says.

I sit on the side facing three big windows—because the seat on this side is higher. The sky turns an off-white. It's now raining.

I open my bag. Where are my questions? I remember picking up the paper, putting it in my binder, and right: I decided not to bring my binder. I text Chris: *I forgot my questions at the hotel.* There's no practical reason for this text except to vent. He replies: *go back!* I tell him it's too late, and he assures me I'll be OK. *You already know what you want to ask him. Plus you'll see him again tomorrow.*

Just then Sarah texts: *Thinking of you!*

I debate whether I should drink. I need to maintain control.

But I order a cocktail anyway, and the server says, That's my favourite.

This reassurance—that I've made a good choice—immediately raises my confidence.

And I still have time. I hurriedly write what questions I remember.

Suddenly Mark approaches. I remain seated. He sits without expecting me to stand. He smiles, and I see where a friend once was.

LIKE A FILM, IN REVERSE

Back at the hotel, I lie in bed, mentally reviewing how I handled my meeting with Mark. I didn't hug him. I was friendly but I pushed back when he, as Sarah would say, started equalising our experiences. I think I talked more than he did. But that's OK. That's more than OK. That's a good thing. Right?

Oh, and right: he acknowledged that he knew, before carrying me into his basement room, that the basement would work to his advantage.

I could reconstruct today's conversation from memory, but I have the audio. I may as well listen to the audio.

Or I could mute his voice. I could just listen to mine. I can handle listening to mine.

Or what if I went hyper-experimental? What if the transcript read something like…

M E: I was hurt, and sort of surprised.

M E: I remember feeling relief that I didn't have to keep this from my dad.

M E: I know so many women who've been sexually assaulted.

I text him: *Thanks for today. It was extraordinarily helpful.*

Mark texts back: *Good! And glad I could help. I kind of felt like I was being really inarticulate, honestly.*

I reply: *I'd feel a little sceptical of flawlessly delivered explanations of sexual assault.*

He texts: *Hah, that's a fair point.*

Instead of thanking him, I should have texted: *Today was useful.* No, that would've been too cold. Or: *I'm glad we met today.* It's so hard not to slip into thinking of him as a friend.

Have I learned nothing from this entire project?

When talking with him, I don't think I used the word *rape*.

Each time I close my eyes, I see the rape. I imagine watching it, like a film, in reverse:

I stop crying. Mark removes his hand from between my legs. He kneels, dresses me slowly. Jake walks down the steps. Together they lift me, carry me upstairs.

But why stop there? Why not rewind until my dad is breathing again?

Cut it out, I tell myself. *Either sleep or work.*

I start transcribing the audio.

...

M E: OK, so it's OK that I'm recording this?
HIM : Yes.
M E: OK. [We laugh nervously.] I think I can black it out. [I turn off the iPad's screen display. Then I turn it back on to confirm the app is still recording.] Yes. It works. OK, so [I turn off the screen]—how have you felt since we last talked?
HIM : It was good to get some of that off my chest. And you actually caught me at a useful time of the year, for

you. Just because I had, in the winter, or February, when we last talked—I'm not as overwhelmed with work. I'm able to be more emotionally present. I actually took a personal day today because I didn't want to come here and be totally fried.

M E: We've talked on the phone, but I haven't seen you in—I guess it's been more than fourteen years.

HIM : It's been an awfully long time.

M E: How have you felt since we last talked on the phone? Has anything changed? Or have you had that experience where you ruminate over something you've said and start to pick it apart?

HIM : I will say I went about sixteen sort of iterations over whether I should offer to pick you up from the airport and then decided not to. [We laugh.]

M E: That's OK. So nothing?

HIM : I don't know how to feel about it.

M E: Let me cover this [I cover the iPad with paper] because this is probably distracting.

HIM : A little bit. [We laugh.] Um. It's just been a strange experience. I think I had buried it a little more than I thought, and so I've been sort of reprocessing my actions—so that was really stressful for a while because I'm basically not happy with who I was. And you know—I don't know. I don't know what to say. I'm glad that you're willing to forgive and move on and this is an interesting project. It's an awkward position to be in, to just be apologising over and over.

M E: It's hard, I would think. I have this concern a lot of the time when I'm writing non-fiction—about authenticity, about being genuine, all while being inventive and reconstructing an experience.

HIM : Well, you'll never be able to write your inner monologue in real time.

ME: Right. [Silence. Server is nearby.] Do you want to order?

HIM: I think I do. Maybe just the cheese plate.

ME: Is here OK? I figured a museum restaurant would be quiet. We can move to a bench or table in the atrium if you want.

HIM: No, this is OK.

ME: OK. So when you were picking apart your memory of that night, I guess that process is a reckoning with your actions and—

HIM: The problem with picking it apart is my memories are so fragmentary. In some ways it feels like it was somebody else. Not to excuse myself. I don't know. I'm having trouble accessing the headspace I was in at that time. It's— [Silence. Server is nearby.] I don't really know what to say.

ME: I understand that you're not trying to excuse it.

HIM: I don't know how to own it and be embarrassed and ashamed of it at the same time. [Server comes. We order.]

ME: You've felt like it wasn't you who—

HIM: I just—and this is not really—it's not just about this incident. It just seems to be how my memory works. I feel like I've done about five different iterations of myself. I was just such a mess as a teenager.

ME: I can understand that.

HIM: The thing that keeps me up at night is I can remember you crying. That's what sticks.

ME: You've said before that this one experience warps your memories of our friendship. For me, I was really worried when I asked you for the five good memories and I hadn't heard from you in a while. I thought, Oh. Maybe this friendship—

HIM: Did we actually never have this friendship?

ME: Yeah, and that was tough for me.

HIM : Coming up with memories, that was harder than I thought.

ME: You sent me a memory of us in Chicago. Was that from our freshman year?

HIM : It must have been. I think it must have been. I remember I hitched a ride with Jake and his uncle. They were going to a football game.

ME: You must have stayed in my dorm.

HIM : Yeah.

ME: Because I was thinking, When did that happen? People think I have a good memory, but I'll insist on never having seen an entire movie and then, right when the credits come on, I'll realise: I have seen this movie before! [We laugh.] I was really happy that you had that memory. And that detail, of us getting lost.

HIM : I was just mortified for days. I really wanted to go to the Skydeck of the Sears Tower and I marched us probably a mile down Michigan Ave in the wrong direction toward the John Hancock Building, and then it was closed. [We laugh.]

ME: I remember we both tried to pretend that what happened hadn't happened. [Server comes, checks in.] I forget where I was going with that. I do remember reaching the point where we stopped talking. My mom would give me updates about you. And, up until then, I had trouble acknowledging that I was angry at you. But then I'd get these updates—because your dad would tell my mom how you were, what you were doing—and I remember feeling indifferent. I remember thinking, Yeah, so? And when I learned you'd dropped out of college, part of me felt bad for you, but another part of me felt indifferent. But now I want you to have a good life. I want you to be happy. And I think that's because this project is giving me closure. That's not necessarily why I'm writing it. But the fact that it's community service in some way. [We laugh.] And before, I tried to rush through the forgiveness process—I forgive you, just read Franny and Zooey and things will be fine—instead of letting myself feel any anger. And by doing that, it wasn't genuine forgiveness. It was Dr Phil forgiveness.

HIM : If you say it enough, you'll believe it.

M E: Or: I'll forgive and I'll just feel better. I was jumping past the emotions, and so there were no negative emotions to overcome. No anger or resentment or whatever. And so, it wasn't real forgiveness, which is probably why I found it hard to move on. And given the years I distanced myself from you, I realise I probably felt contempt. But now, I don't know—to know that you've felt bad about it, I find that helpful. And that you acknowledged it was bad, that has been helpful to me—in processing some of this. For years I thought, Maybe it wasn't that bad.

HIM : Jesus.

M E: Well no, but really.

HIM : I get the rationalisation process there, but just—it's one of those things that I regret you had to go through that process let alone—[His voice trails off.]

M E: I remember after it happened, Amber saying—she was really upset—saying, Jeannie, that was rape, and I said, No, it wasn't. And then Jake finding out. And then the masculinity, the impulse toward violence, coming out. Jake saying, I'm going to kick his ass. That was another question I wanted to ask you: with Jake—you were never a bro-y guy. Do you think that living in that house with Jake—I remember posters of women in bikinis. I definitely remember *Maxim*s and *Playboy*s.

HIM : Jake and his uncle had their whole little bro-fantasy thing going on.

M E: Did that influence you?

HIM : I don't—I mean, yes, it's probably fair to say that it would have. I don't feel like I was ever that guy. But, I mean, I may not be in the most objective position on that.

M E: Well, you said that what had happened changed the sort of narrative you could tell about yourself. You used to think of yourself as one of the good guys. Who were the bad guys, would you say? Who would you envision?

HIM : Semi-serious answer: [name of high school football player].

M E: I completely forgot about him. Oh man, yeah, yeah, OK. What about him? Why?

HIM : He had this casual indifference toward the idea of learning about anything. He just—he was everything I didn't want to be in high school. And he was also more popular. Not to drag up twenty-year-old high school drama. I really couldn't stand that guy.

M E: Yeah, I completely forgot about him. So he was one of the bad guys.

HIM : He actually seems like he's grown up to be—he's actually a teacher in Sandusky now or something. For whatever that's worth.

M E: There were some great teachers. But then there was my newspaper adviser. You knew something had happened between him and me, but you didn't know what.

HIM : I never got a straight answer out of anybody. There was gossip that something had happened.

M E: I remember your dad—and this is a weird thing to remember—but there was something involving a mini-fridge. Your dad wouldn't return a mini-fridge to my adviser, or he wouldn't loan a mini-fridge to him. Your dad told me, I don't like him anymore. And that meant so much to me—because there were some teachers who seemed to be on my adviser's side. I'd see them

241

laughing with him in the hallways. So, you didn't know about my adviser. We never talked about him. The fact that we didn't—the fact that you didn't know what had happened. I'm surprised I didn't confide in you. Recently that made me question my understanding of our friendship, which I really didn't want to question. Though I didn't confide in a lot of people I cared about. And I mean, of course the assault made me question our friendship. But also: the fact that the assault happened surrounding the one-year anniversary of my dad's death. You knew I was upset about my dad. And it was the first time I'd been drunk. I was definitely vulnerable, and—

HIM : And I preyed on that vulnerability.

M E: Yeah.

HIM : I don't think I fully appreciated at the time the extent to which you were having trouble dealing with your dad's death. I don't recall a calculation that I made, that like: this is my plan and I'm going to—she is in this vulnerable state and this is my opportunity to take advantage. Not to say that that would have been beyond me. But I don't recall having that train of thought. But yeah, it's just—it just makes me feel that much worse—about the timing of it. Not—I don't know how to say it. There is just no polite way to talk about some of this. I don't know. It's one of those details that I don't think I appreciated at the time. But looking at it, in retrospect, from your perspective, it's just more heartbreaking.

M E: We would talk on the phone for hours after he died, and you remembered that fact. You knew, had to have known, I was devastated about my dad's death. So—what was our friendship? Were we? Did you think of us as friends?

HIM : Yeah, I thought of us as really close friends and also—there's no nice way to put it: I was in love with you as a person, the idea I had constructed of you. Which probably makes it worse, not better.

M E: What was the idea of me?

HIM : Just, we never had the relationship. I never had an intimate knowledge of your inner personality.

M E: My inner personality?

HIM : It's tough to be in love with somebody you're not—people don't generally throw that word around. And it's not generally with people they talk on the phone with an hour at a time. [Server brings us drinks.]

TRYING TO TORTURE YOURSELF MUCH?

It's nine-thirty in the morning, and Mark and I are at a café in his neighbourhood. I decide against recording the conversation. Last night he seemed a little tense, which I appreciated. If the rape were easy for him to talk about, I'd be hurt. But I want him to loosen up a bit. Recording the conversation gets in the way of that. Also, some part of me wants to pretend we're two friends simply catching up.

I give him some old photos, and he smiles, looking at them. One is of him, Amber, my first boyfriend, and me dressed for homecoming. Another is of him and Amber at homecoming. And the last one is of him, his dad, and his brother clumped together on their family room couch.

I feel bad, I tell him, that I haven't seen your parents in so long.

I think they'd be really happy to hear from you, he says. I don't think my mom would hold it against you anymore.

Anymore? I ask.

It's been such a long time, he says.

I wonder if Mark registers how odd that'd be—for me to visit his parents and pretend that the rape hadn't happened, hadn't been the reason I stopped talking to them. I don't tell him that, though. And I don't press him on whether or not his mom indeed held my silence against me.

Instead, I tell him that I've tried to think of terrible things I've done to people.

I slept with a man who had a girlfriend, I tell Mark. I'd never met her. But I knew he was dating someone. And I slept with him anyway. He lived in London but whenever he visited New York I'd drop everything to see him. I've felt bad about it for a long time now.

And on the other side of that, he says, I never told you my feelings because you were dating someone. I was trying to respect that. I regret never telling you that I liked you.

Does he believe that had he shared his feelings, we would be together now?

Does *what could have been* remain alive in his mind?

But I don't ask him.

For the next five hours, we reminisce about high school, mostly. We discuss politics. We discuss our jobs. We discuss books we've both read.

I still have my copy of *Franny and Zooey*, he says. I see it every day. My bookshelf is right by my bed.

He says that my first book is on his coffee table.

Trying to torture yourself much? I ask him, and we both laugh.

Mark then reminds me that he'll never forget my crying.

When I think about that night, he says, I think about how what happened was already in my mind before I carried you into my room.

He said the same thing last night, and I still don't know how to respond. I look at my watch. I can't look at Mark. I know the rape will always stalk the outskirts of our conversations.

I should head to the airport, I tell him.

We both walk outside. While waiting for my cab, we talk about how strange this all is.

I'll leave out identifying details, I tell him. But anyone who knew us, they'd be able to figure it out.

That's OK, he says.

Really? I ask him.

Yeah. Also, I don't mean to tell you how to do your project, but don't go too easy on me. I know you want it to be nuanced, but I don't really deserve that. There's no excuse for what I did.

He looks like he might cry. My cab pulls up, and I surprise myself by hugging him.

I call Leigh-Anne from the airport.

Mark said he sort of knew that if he could get me into the basement, it would be to his advantage.

Wow, she says. I didn't think he'd admit that. How do you feel?

Numb. I don't know. I hugged him. I don't know why I hugged him.

It's OK, she says.

Something he said this morning has been bothering me. I told him that one of the worst things I've ever done is sleep with a guy who had a girlfriend. And Mark told me that on the reverse side of that, he didn't tell me his feelings for me when we were teenagers because he was trying to respect that I was dating someone.

But you didn't sexually assault somebody, Leigh-Anne tells me. You had consensual sex. That's very different.

Thank you for talking me through all of this.

Of course, she says.

As the plane lifts into the sky, I think: *our secrets make us human.*

Knock off the sentimentality, I tell myself.

Window seats always make me sentimental. I put on my headphones and start transcribing.

...

M E: Going back to Jake. Jake knew what had happened, but he never followed up with me. But you said he went down to the basement to make sure you weren't breaking things.

HIM : That was basically as far as it went. I was never— Jake and I had a very adversarial relationship. We had known one another since kindergarten. And for most of that time, we hated each other. Or at least I hated him.

M E: Really?

HIM : He used to bully me when we were in second grade.

M E: Jake was a bully?

HIM : Yeah, he was an asshole. He always has been an asshole. He is an asshole today.

M E: He is?

HIM : I mean, I haven't talked to him in a decade, but— [His voice trails off.]

M E: I hadn't known that whole backstory. I didn't know he ever bullied you.

HIM : I mean, we're bringing up ancient history now. But yeah, suffice to say I hated Jake's guts for most of my childhood. And then we sort of reconciled as teenagers. And then, I don't know. It was the best of several bad options, to live with him and his uncle.

M E: I only met his uncle—that was the first time, I think, and I remember he showed me a *Playboy*, an issue from the sixties or seventies, and he made some comment about how back then women didn't wax, and I thought, Is he trying to show some progressive belief about women's body hair? Because if that's the case, women's facial hair, now that would be progressive.

HIM : I like a woman with a moustache. [We laugh.]

M E: I was trying to run through the different people who were there that night. Amber and Jake and Garrett. I think Garrett tried to get me to stop drinking.

HIM : Sounds like the kind of thing he might have done.

M E: Garrett always seemed like a really decent, really good guy. I heard he's a scientist.

HIM : I think he worked for NASA for a while. I think he's out in Arizona or something.

M E: This must have been five or six years ago, but he was visiting New York when I lived there, and he wanted to meet up. But I didn't, or couldn't. I think I wasn't feeling well, adjusting to new meds or something. I've regretted that. Because I did think of him as a good friend. And then we fell out of touch, which was my fault. And recently, I've been thinking about Daniel.

HIM : We were good—well, our parents were good friends. And so we would hang out when our parents would hang out. We were never that close. But I like Daniel.

M E: He got married.

HIM : Yeah, he lives in the suburbs.

M E: This would have been in college—I don't think you were there—but I visited his house. Maybe it's the same one. It was in the suburbs. He was married by that point. Or engaged. A bunch of us went. And I remember we were all sleeping on his living room floor. Were you there?

HIM : I don't think so.

M E: He woke me up, to see if I wanted to have sex with him. And I said, You're married. Or: You're engaged. His wife or fiancée was in the other room.

HIM : Your wife is six feet away from us.

M E: Yeah, and I don't remember if I left then. I was so upset. I'm almost sure that this happened later in college, after the assault. And I remember thinking, Male friendships. Are they possible? They feel impossible.

HIM : Like, What are we even doing?

M E: Yeah. Carlos, though, he was always a good guy.

HIM : Yeah, Carlos was. Still is. Aside from you now, he's the only person from high school I'm still in touch with.

M E: I could be wrong here, but I sensed that Carlos may have felt pressure to be extra good—because of race. His father was black and his mother was—Puerto Rican?

HIM : Yeah. Puerto Rican.

M E: How much do you think that race factors into this narrative? The narrative of what happened between us?

HIM : In what way?

M E: You mentioned that you used to steal things, little things, to see what you could get away with. And I'm wondering if you—maybe not consciously—thought you were above—

HIM : I definitely thought I was above every single rule ever made.

M E: Why?

HIM : Part of it was me just being oppositionally defiant, in general. Part of it was me being a teenager, seeing what rules he could actually break. A lot of it was ego trip stuff, which I think is not uncommon with gifted children. It's just, you think you're smarter than everybody else and the rules don't apply to you. I don't feel like I'm that unique in that regard.

M E: Do you think that coloured what happened with us?

BUT I JUST ENDED UP FEELING NUMB

Chris picks me up at the Baltimore airport. I tell him that I hugged Mark.

That's OK, Chris says. I feel like the natural instinct is to hug somebody you were friends with for years.

Yeah, I say. I wanted to demonstrate that I do forgive him. It felt right to do, or I thought it did, anyway. But I just ended up feeling numb afterward. Oh, and he said that he thought his parents would be happy to hear from me. But why would I contact his parents? He doesn't want them to find out. Does he think I can compartmentalise like that?

Him suggesting that, Chris says, that you talk to his family as if everything is OK, it confirms something.

What's that?

That it's easier for the guilty person to move on, or at least to pretend it didn't happen. It's harder for the innocent person.

At home, after dinner with Chris, I return to the recording.

...

HIM : Probably. Not that I thought I was entitled to do that. That being my general mode, I'm sure, had an influence.

M E: On the phone you mentioned: I knew what I was doing was wrong while I was doing it and I did it anyway. What got you to that point? I've asked you this before, I think, but: why didn't you stop? Can you try to answer that?

HIM : Not the easiest question to answer. I wish I could tie it up in a little bow for you. Though in general I don't believe in tying things up in bows.

M E: It's a hard question.

HIM : Why did you rape me when you knew you probably shouldn't?

M E: OK, so this interests me: you use the word. And I know that the word fits the definition. And we've talked about this: how it's helpful that such actions do fit the definition. Because at the time the reason—not the only reason—but one reason I didn't report it was, I didn't believe it qualified as rape.

HIM : And I had never really considered it rape until you made that point. I'm also not going to intentionally sugarcoat it. The word fits the crime.

M E: Earlier this week, I was visiting my friend Nina, whose ex-boyfriend blackmailed her into rape. For several years she didn't think it qualified as rape. She didn't push him away. But he had a video of them having sex, from when they were dating, and he threatened to send it to her parents if she didn't have sex with him again. And she comes from a very traditional Indian family. Her parents believed she was still a virgin. So she ended up blaming herself: for lying to her parents about being a virgin, for the video existing, for not pushing him away, for cheating on this guy when they were together. That's why he was mad. When I first met her, we were roommates in the psych ward, and she told me what her ex had done, how he'd threatened to send the tape to her parents, and I told her, He blackmailed you into sex. That's rape. And the way she talked about it—I thought the rape had just happened. Turns out it had happened three years prior. I told her that I probably would handle that situation differently now. Instead of immediately saying, That's rape, I might try to help her arrive at that conclusion. But she said she was glad I'd called it rape. No one who knew about it—except for maybe her sister—had labelled it rape. I guess what I'm trying to say is: I don't want my use of the word to be disrespectful to women whose experiences with rape are more serious than my experience with you. Of course, when I told that to Nina, she laughed and said I was being ridiculous. [We laugh.] She said that of course she didn't find it offensive or disrespectful.

HIM : Sounds right.

ONLY BECAUSE HE OWES THAT TO ME

Nina calls, coincidentally, while I'm transcribing my description of her situation.

I am so sorry, she says. I had a friend's bachelorette party in New Orleans.

Sorry for what? I say.

I didn't call you after your trip to see Mark.

I didn't expect you to call right away, I tell her. And it's only been a couple of days since I visited.

But I've been thinking of you. Tell me: how was it?

I summarise the visit and then ask Nina how she's doing.

No, she says. We are talking about you. I want to hear more about the visit. How did you feel after the second day seeing him?

Empty, I say. I thought I'd feel differently, but after I said goodbye and got in the cab, I felt wiped.

That makes sense, Nina says. There was so much buildup. And then, what more could he tell you?

I don't want this to be a one-sided conversation, I say. How are you doing?

Nina laughs.

Nothing interesting is happening with me right now, she says. How are you feeling now? Are you still feeling empty?

Sort of. Empty and stuck. Ever since I got back, it's been hard to write.

As a reader, Nina says, I would want to know if your views about the friendship have changed.

That's a good question, I tell her. I haven't yet written about that.

Have your views changed?

I don't know. Friendships are founded on intimate bonds and trust. Sort of like how you and I quickly became friends in the psych ward, fast-forwarding to the deep, serious stuff. So with Mark, it's as if we're becoming friends again, forging this deep bond based on this horrible act that he's afraid to talk about with anyone else. But I'm not going to be friends with Mark. That'd be impossible at this point. He and I are having this intimate conversation, but only because he owes that to me. Do you think you would ever confront your ex about what he did?

No, definitely not. I've been thinking about that, actually. I never want to see him again.

. . .

ME: Nina is one of my closest friends. And I feel fortunate—because I have so many great female friendships. But in high school, I remember, I used to pride myself on being friends with guys.

HIM: Trying to be a cool girl has been toxic for any number of people over the years.

ME: Yeah. I tried not to seem like I cared about my clothes and hair and make-up—at least not as much as the other girls. I used to think the other girls were occupied with concerns far less important than *Quake* and *Counter-Strike*. [We laugh.] I didn't even like those games. [We laugh.] But I have such great female friendships now, and a lot of that is because we're so open with one another. We confide in one another. We help one another through tough situations. I don't know how I could live without those friendships. You mentioned you don't have close friendships.

HIM : I'm not in that position. And there are any number of reasons for it. My health has not been great. Mentally or physically. And I don't—I've never been able to make friends with men. I don't like most of the things that other guys like. I'm not—I find it hard to say this. This is more of a therapist conversation than this kind of conversation. But I got to a point where I just had to shut everything out in order to keep my head above water, and I still find myself doing that, and it inhibits me from—it kills joy. It keeps me alive, but also I have trouble experiencing joy in things, which is not great for socialising.

M E: Have you thought about getting a therapist since we last talked? I know we talked about it briefly before.

HIM : It's one of those things I probably should do but obstinately won't do.

M E: Why? It seems like now—it's obviously your decision. But it seems like it could help.

HIM : Part of it is the expense. I have health insurance but it's not particularly great health insurance. I'm sure seeing a therapist is fairly expensive. It's also, I don't know how comfortable I am—in some ways I feel like I can talk about this with you—like I owe that to you in a way, but I don't owe that to a therapist. Generally speaking, I don't know that I really want to have that conversation with a stranger.

M E: OK. Though a therapist would owe it to you to listen. Maybe you could find a sliding-scale therapist. It might be hard. But you could do it, I think.

HIM : I haven't explored it.

M E: I Skype with my therapist every week, and it's been really helpful. I met him in New York six or seven years ago. Before seeing him, I used to be anti. [Server checks on us.] But yeah, I've found it helpful. I imagine that these conversations—they've been hard for you but also—

HIM : Yeah, I got—I mean, I had a minor depressive episode surrounding—which is fine, but you know, I was sort of reprocessing a lot of this stuff, and that was difficult. Our last conversation didn't feel like closure exactly, but it was helpful.

M E: What about it didn't feel like closure?

HIM : Part of that is just me being bad at closure. I sort of have this masochistic streak where I should be punishing myself more.

M E: Your parents don't know about the assault. You said your sister sort of knows. She knows something happened.

HIM : I don't know that she knows any details. I think Amber told her that—you'd have to ask Amber what she told her.

M E: I think I told you this, but last time I talked to Amber, she didn't remember what had happened.

HIM : OK, fair enough.

M E: And then that was when I thought maybe it wasn't a big deal. Oh—this reminds me, I actually brought something. [I look through my bag.]

HIM : And now I'm the asshole with no gift. [We laugh.]

M E: No, no. You know what, I think I left—I'll bring them tomorrow. I have photos for you—ones from high school. But I left them at the hotel with my questions, actually. Circling back, your sister, she vaguely knew what happened. But your parents—and by the way, I would never tell your parents. You have a good relationship with your dad now. What would—

HIM : He would—it would destroy him. It would destroy our relationship.

M E: Again, I'm not going to tell them.

HIM : I appreciate that. In some ways, it's like a reckoning that never happened. That I just lucked out of. What will be will be.

SO MUCH WORK

Adam asks me if I have a specific readership in mind.

I'd like the book to reach a wide audience, I tell him, but I'm guessing it will attract mostly women. I definitely want it to reach college students.

What is the message, Adam asks me, that you want these young women to walk away with? If it had to be synthesised.

Don't worry about protecting the guy who assaulted you. Don't worry about the feelings of the guy's family or friends. Your job is not to protect them. He screwed up. He messed up those relationships, not you. And yet, here I am, not talking to Mark's family. Part of that is fourteen years have passed. Part of that is it'd be so much work. It's so much work to come forward. And yet a lot of people blame the victims for not reporting sexual assault, as if it's entirely their responsibility to rid the world of rapists.

We get seduced, right? Adam says. We end up identifying with the aggressor. We'll get angry with the victim because she's not doing the work of coming forward. It's her not doing something that's a problem again. I think of getting into a car accident, that analogy. If my hands are on the wheel, ten and two, and I'm obeying the law and somebody just whizzes through a light and T-bones me, I have to go to the hospital. I have to file the insurance claim. I have to do physical therapy. I have to go to psychotherapy. And I didn't do anything. Even if the person who caused the accident, even if that person goes to physical therapy, it's not going to improve my hip. Emotions aside—which this primarily is—but organising your time, taking your time to talk to his parents, for example: who cares to do that? It's work. Why should you have to be the one? It's very twisted.

...

M E: I always thought of your dad as a feminist.

HIM : Yeah, as much as a child who grew up in the seventies can be. He's really liberal.

M E: There weren't many progressive men in Sandusky.

HIM : There's definitely an absence. It's a pretty conservative town.

M E: Which is why I liked talking with your dad so much. He seemed very open-minded.

HIM : He is. And more so than he would let on when we were in high school—because he was also a principal and had to maintain a reputation, which he would never stop reminding me.

M E: Right, because when he caught you with porn.

HIM : That was the reason he cited for why I couldn't look at porn. Not just because it's wrong but because: it would also be bad for your father.

M E: Thinking back to the non-progressiveness of the men you lived with, I remember feeling disappointed that Jake never reached out to me. Nobody really did.

HIM : I feel like we all fell into this agreement: let's not talk about it and it will go away. Which probably is not the healthiest way of dealing with that.

M E: In undergrad, when I met with campus therapists, they often asked if I'd been sexually assaulted, and I always replied, Yeah, but that's not what I'm here for. Because the assault seemed like such a distraction, which is a weird way of thinking about it. But it did seem like a distraction.

HIM : That had to have been difficult—because you were dealing with other legitimate problems, and this was one more antagonistic thing to add to the pile.

M E: And my first boyfriend, I think he shaped my understanding—or influenced my understanding—of how relationships should go. I don't know if I ever talked about this, but, when he was mad at me, he would get horrible road rage. To the point that I thought he'd kill us. After I broke up with him, in Chicago, he gunned it toward a busy intersection, and I had to lie: I love you, I love you, let's talk about this at my dorm. And so I didn't feel like I had a great view of men after everything.

HIM : Understandably so.

M E: How has the experience influenced—so you haven't dated anyone. Have you had crushes?

HIM : Yeah, I mean, I've had a couple situations of unrequited crushes, which typically I end up detonating at some point by writing a really embarrassing email or text message and getting completely shut down.

M E: Co-workers? People in school?

HIM : Usually friends. I mean, how open are you to someone you've been friends with for two or three years suddenly sending you an email that's dumping out their—it's not the best move.

M E: So you did try and take certain friendships to a new level?

HIM : Yeah. But I'm too chickenshit to do it at a point where I might actually have a chance at success. I don't know. It's fine.

M E: Do your parents ever talk about wanting—

HIM : They've given up on me. [We laugh.] After they got amazing grandkids from my sister, the pressure was off.

M E: And your brother, is he with anyone?

HIM : He's not.

M E: How often do you talk to him?

HIM : Pretty much on a daily basis. He's my only male friend. Well, Carlos is a friend, but we don't talk as much. I have a good relationship with my brother. We just don't talk about feelings. We talk exclusively about bullshit.

M E: You told him we were in touch.

HIM : I mentioned a few months ago that I had heard from you. That's about it.

M E: What scares you, other than somebody figuring out your identity? What scares you the most about this project?

HIM : Obviously it's not a flattering portrait of me. [We laugh.] Which is fine. There's a little bit of existential dread into just how unflattering it will end up reading.

M E: So you do plan to read it?

HIM : Yeah, I mean, at this point I'm invested. [We laugh.] Unless you don't want me to.

M E: No, no, no. Of course I'm OK with you reading it. And if I were you, I'd be curious. I think what's been interesting for me is that I think of so many good memories of us, and I'm writing those as well. I think that's what makes it—

HIM : The Greek tragedy aspect of it?

M E: Nuanced—for me, at least. With my first boyfriend, I would not be able to find nuance or be civil or whatever. But now I'm thinking of the friend who raped me in New York. While that friendship meant less—which is probably why I'm not writing too much about that experience—I see a lot of nuance there. Five or so months after the rape, he called me. We were still sort of talking, pretending that what happened hadn't happened. And we had the same friend circle, which made things uncomfortable. But anyway, he and I were sort of trying to be friends again. He called. He sensed that I'd been feeling off—feeling drastically up and then drastically down. And when I answered, I was slurring my words. I'd just taken all the pills in my apartment. Some of which turned out to be methadone. Who knew that when you order prescription drugs from an online Canadian pharmacy, it'd be methadone? [We laugh.] So he probably saved my life by calling. He hurried over and got me to a hospital. Looking back, I feel torn between anger and gratitude. He raped me. But he saved my life. And then here's where the mental health aspect figures into this project. My diagnosis—my history of mania and depression and psychosis—it marks me as an unreliable narrator. Even before the diagnosis, I felt like I came across as unreliable. I remember reading the police reports about the situation with my newspaper adviser. I remember reading them back then and thinking, Wow, this girl, me, does not come across as trustworthy.

HIM: But that's because of whoever the asshole was who wrote that report.

ME: Right. But it's hard to confront the mental health aspect of this story. Do you think of yourself as an unreliable narrator?

HIM: I mean, in general, a little bit, and about this specific instance: yes.

ME: OK, how so?

HIM: Well, just— [Server interrupts, tells us the kitchen is about to close.]

ME: OK, so you do think of yourself as an unreliable narrator.

HIM: I wasn't quite blackout drunk, but I was close. And my memory about—I have a really excellent memory about particular things, and everything else that doesn't stick just goes.

M E: You say you were almost blackout drunk, but you do remember a lot of the night. You remembered a lot of it in detail.

HIM : I wasn't blackout drunk, but I was pretty drunk.

M E: In discussing this, do you feel like an unreliable narrator?

HIM : In terms of second-guessing my own motivations for the claims?

M E: Yeah.

HIM : I'm making the attempt not to be in that regard. The success of that attempt is open to interpretation. I'm doing my best to explain what I remember without twisting it in my favour, because I don't feel like that's—that would feel unbecoming. But, yeah— am I doing that unconsciously? Possibly. Probably, even.

M E: You said you didn't feel like you deserved forgiveness, and maybe you still don't feel that way. But this, what you're doing—if there was ever any way to make amends, it would definitely be this. Sure, had this never happened, I'd be working on something else. But still, your participation means a lot.

HIM : I'm glad.

M E: I'm saving you lots of money with therapy, I guess. [We laugh.]

HIM : Why get therapy when you can just wait fifteen years? [We laugh.]

M E: When you talk to your brother—you talk every day. Do you talk on the phone?

HIM : Mostly text.

M E: I'm such a phone person.

HIM : There is almost nothing I would rather do. Talking on the phone is my least favourite thing in the world to do.

M E: Why is that?

HIM : I don't know exactly. I'm bad at it. Which I think in itself would be a reason for me. But I just don't like doing it. I don't know that there's a rational reason; actually, talking on the phone is stupid for these seven reasons. [We laugh.] But it viscerally is something I don't like doing.

M E: I know you don't like talking on the phone, but still: I'm sorry I fell out of touch after our last phone call.

HIM : No, it wasn't your job to be my social life.

M E: I know. I know. But then I recently noticed that you'd sent me a nice text message and I never replied to it.

HIM : I was never mad about that.

M E: It's been a busy semester. I was trying to be extra present for students. My student who killed herself, she's really been on my mind.

HIM : It's a tragic story and we're talking about basically the same issue.

M E: I was so naive to think she was over the rape. I don't know if I fully believed she was.

HIM : But at a certain point you can't make people ask for help.

M E: A lot of the time she seemed happy. She'd joke with me. Meanwhile, I was really worried about her friend who'd been recently raped. She also took my class, and she seemed suicidal. It's just, the number of rape essays I read every semester. It's hard.

HIM : I'm sure. As a creative writing professor.

M E: Teaching creative non-fiction, teaching memoir, I learn so much about my students. They really open up. And I'm glad they feel they can trust me with their stories. But it can get emotionally exhausting. I recently looked around my office and realised that all the gifts from former students were from students who'd been raped. One student knit me a scarf. Looking at it recently,

I remembered her story: how the guy put something in her drink before he raped her. He must have drugged her—because she woke up with bruises, was partially undressed, and the last thing she remembered was sipping from a single glass of wine. And two other students, they mailed me a vintage typewriter from Portland. Both of them had been raped. One of them came to me the day after she'd been raped. She didn't want her boyfriend to find out because she thought he'd blame her. Other guys in the frat had watched it happen.

JUST VISITING AN OLD FRIEND

I can't hold my students' rapists accountable. And I can't bring myself to hold Mark accountable. I don't know what accountability would look like at this point. This project isn't it. It's actually helping him. Which is probably why I told him about my students. Because I don't want him to reach complete catharsis.

I'm at the salon for a root touch-up. And this is how I know I've made it. I used to buy drugstore hair dye and hope for the best. It was fun, though, not to know what colour I would really get.

My stylist asks about my weekend.

I just got back from Ohio, I say—and immediately regret mentioning it.

What were you doing in Ohio? she asks.

Right now I wish I could do small talk. I wonder, though, what is medium talk?

Just visiting an old friend, I say.

I tell Chris how hard it is to talk to acquaintances lately.

If somebody asks what I'm working on, I don't know what to say. Telling the truth borders on rude. But being vague also feels rude.

Why is it rude, he asks, to say what your book is about?

Because who wants to enter a conversation about sexual assault?

But isn't that the point? Chris says. You're writing this because people should be talking about it.

Sure. But am I supposed to describe the book to my hairstylist?

Why not?

It's not rude?

No. Not at all.

...

HIM : That just—I understand how women can come to that frame of reasoning. But that kind of stuff drives me totally insane.

M E: This concern—even when I look back over the transcripts of our conversations, there are times I see myself being overly reassuring. I said things like, I hope you know I'm not mad at you. I hope this is helping you. And so on. I've probably already done it in this conversation. There is this desire to make men happy. Or to not upset men.

HIM : It's just a social conditioning thing.

M E: Yeah.

HIM : Neither here nor there, but could the insanity that is incels happen at a more opportune time for the purposes of this project?

M E: What are your thoughts on that?

HIM : I don't recognise these people. I don't understand it at all. And I feel like I'm in a position to. But I don't. I try not to do hatred—because it just doesn't work for me. But the contempt these men have for all women—I just don't, I don't understand it.

M E: These guys—a lot of them are on Reddit. I've never used Reddit. Do you ever use those sites, the ones that these angry incel guys are ruining?

HIM : I was pretty active on Reddit for a number of years, but that was before, mostly before—this is going a little Internet nerd, but Reddit circa 2004, 2005, was mostly disaffected grad students and college types. It was bro-y even then, but it wasn't the right-wing troll factory that it is now. Which happened because at 4chan—which is where all those people used to post—there was some crackdown. There was drama with that website, and so there was this mass exodus from 4chan to Reddit, and within the space of maybe a month, the culture at Reddit completely changed.

M E: One of my students mentioned 4chan to me, and I didn't know what he was talking about. I asked him what it was, and he claimed it's really very nice.

HIM : It's not. It was never. 4chan was the place where every troll-y right-wing meme originated, ever. It was just a place for people to be awful to each other, for fun. And also to share anime porn.

M E: So you don't really use Reddit—

HIM : I haven't really been an active Redditer in, I don't know, two to three years. The last several years I had been on Reddit I was mostly answering questions in AskScience.

M E: I know there's a cute animal section on Reddit—because friends will send me photos from that. That's useful, actually. [We laugh.]

HIM : There are two or three good subreddits that are just cute animal pictures. And the rest is mostly awful.

M E: You mention incels and that whole movement, how it's been in the news more. And then #MeToo is happening.

HIM : The intersection of the #MeToo movement being so public and then you contacting me—and then I read your book and felt horrible and—it was just like, for about a month, every time I would see a #MeToo story, it felt like it was about me personally. Which is reductive or whatever. It was probably healthy in shaping the reprocessing or reckoning with what had happened, in retrospect. So maybe that's good.

M E: Do you and your brother ever discuss #MeToo?

HIM : We pretty much talk about NBA Twitter exclusively. And whatever ridiculous thing Trump is doing that day.

M E: I guess it's NBA trade rumour time.

HIM : Yeah, we're heading into free agency and the draft was yesterday. I follow the NBA pretty closely. I'm a serial obsessive. For two or three years, I'll be fixated on one subject, and so between '07 and 2010 or so, that was mostly the NBA.

M E: So you're into sports.

HIM : I am exclusively into the NBA. And mostly I got really into NBA analytics—because of course I did, because I'm a huge nerd.

M E: So you and your brother haven't discussed #MeToo. But your dad, has he talked about it?

HIM : Those aren't conversations we're really equipped to have. I get the general sense that he's very supportive, but where he's at in terms of his own personal reckoning, I couldn't tell you. He is the most conscientiously ethical man I've ever met. It's really important to him to do the right thing by people in every conceivable circumstance.

M E: How much do you think about—not to sound too academic, but ideas of masculinity—

HIM : And the curse that is toxic masculinity and so forth? I mean, I wouldn't say I spend a great deal of time thinking about it, but more just when I—it occurs to me more when I meet other men, and I'm just like: why? I was actually driving with my dad to Lowe's or something to pick up God knows what. And we were sitting at the stoplight next to these forty-five-year-old biker guys in the big leather vests— [Server comes, checks in on us. I order another drink.]

M E: So you guys were at a light next to—

HIM: Yeah, just some biker guys in the Harleys with the loud exhaust, and I don't know. I got viscerally angry, like: why would you put on this whole costume and pretend to be a badass when you know you're an accountant who does nothing? The whole fantasy I don't understand.

M E: And thinking of toxic masculinity, I mean: how about Jake's uncle's house?

HIM: Sure, that's completely fair.

HEREIN LIES THE TRAGEDY

I'm reviewing the transcripts in a gluten-free, vegan café in a trendy Baltimore neighbourhood when a man comes in wearing an attitude shirt: *GOT MANHOOD?* He walks past my table and I turn and see the back of his shirt: *Herein lies the tragedy of the age: not that men are wicked but that men know so little of men. —W. E. B. Du Bois.*

I Google *Herein lies the tragedy of the age* and find the full quote (which wouldn't have fit well on the back of a T-shirt): *Herein lies the tragedy of the age: not that men are poor,—all men know something of poverty; not that men are wicked,—who is good? not that men are ignorant,—what is Truth? Nay, but that men know so little of men.*

I think of Mark's clichéd notion of toxic masculinity. The point of this project is to show what seemingly nice guys are capable of.

...

M E: Did the conversations that happened—

HIM : Jake's uncle was a pig. He was all, Bitches this and women are the worst and this is why. He was the worst.

M E: And you and Jake—

HIM : We were barely friends when I was living with him. And a year or two of living with him was enough. I haven't talked to him in probably—not quite as long as since I last saw you, but pretty close. At least a decade.

M E: You were pretty depressed while living there. And you were depressed in high school certainly. How much do you think that factored into what happened?

HIM: Oh, that was definitely part of it. I was right at the cusp of a breaking point in general. And some of that ended up focusing on you. I think I said this a little bit earlier, but I always just assumed I would kill myself at some point. I think it wasn't until my mid-twenties when I decided, No, I think I'm going to stick around.

M E: I was thinking about how—

HIM: And—oh, go ahead.

M E: No. It's OK.

HIM: I'm curious about what you're—

M E: When I think back to that time, I was in a bad place as well.

HIM: Yeah, we were miserable together. [Server interrupts, checks on us.]

M E: We were both depressed, sure. But why do you think you acted in that way in your depression?

HIM: I don't think it had that much to do with you— other than you were in my line of fire, so to speak. But yeah, and especially at nineteen when you're pumped full of hormones and not sleeping at night. I don't know if I could construct a narrative where it makes sense that this happened, but I do feel like it was part and parcel of what happened.

M E: I'm trying to think of the worst act I've committed when depressed. Far more men than women commit sexual assault.

HIM: Sure.

M E: I guess what I'm—I don't know what I'm asking.

HIM: Why did I convert angst into sexual assault?

M E: Yeah.

HIM: It's a good question. Especially at that age, it was more important to me to—it used to really bother me as I got—when I was college-age—that I hadn't been in a relationship, hadn't had sex. That used to make me angrier than it does now. So that was probably part of it.

ME: Do you think if it hadn't been me? If it had been someone else in the friend group. Amber, for example?

HIM: Do you mean: can I envision a scenario where this happened but it was Amber and not you?

ME: Or any other woman?

HIM: I think possibly other than—you remember earlier when I was talking about making embarrassing confessions? I'd already done that with Amber at one point. And it ended ugly.

ME: How did she handle it?

HIM: She shut me down pretty hard. Which is fine. But I don't know that I took it particularly well. As I recall, I wrote her some ridiculously embarrassing email.

ME: Was it around that time?

HIM: No, this would have been at least a year or so before.

ME: It's been so long that it's hard to reconstruct, but the one thing that confuses me—

HIM: OK—

ME: Why carry me into the basement? That's the one thing—I don't really remember the house that well.

HIM: If I'm being totally honest, this is a two-part answer. One, yes, I used to hang out with people in the basement. I had a computer down there and we'd watch movies. Two— [Server brings me another cocktail, takes away our plates.]

ME: So you were saying, one, you would go down there—

AND HE'S DOING THIS WILLINGLY?

Chris and I are drinking with friends on a back deck lit with string lights. The house belongs to a couple we're just getting to know. Almost everybody here writes. One guy served in the air force and now works at a recycling plant.

This professional recycler, I worry, feels bored by our writerly discussions about the revision process. Also, he is the only guest without a significant other. So I ask him about recycling. How much should we clean our jars and bottles before dumping them into a recycling bin? And are the caps really OK to recycle? Why are some yogurt containers not recyclable? Or has this policy changed? Why do some companies allow for paper and plastic to mix? Chris, the guy who lives here, and I listen to his explanations. The others, on the other side of the deck, discuss an editor who shut down his poetry press after multiple sexual assault allegations were made against him. One of the poets here, a friend, lost two books. Her second book was forthcoming from that press. Her first book, as a result of the press shutting down, will soon be out of print.

And he never apologised, she explains.

The guy who lives here, he's also a poet. He asks me what I'm working on these days.

I look at Chris, and Chris says, It's really interesting.

I hesitate, hedge, say, It comes out next year.

The poet and professional recycler are looking at me, expecting more.

I'm interviewing a guy, I explain, who sexually assaulted me fourteen years ago. We used to be friends, but obviously the friendship couldn't survive.

And he's doing this willingly? the poet asks. Talking to you?

Yeah, I was sort of surprised.

Wow, the recycler says.

That is interesting, the poet says. You know, my brother, he raped someone. This was years ago. It's hard to talk about. I'm still upset about it.

Do you and your brother, I begin—but I don't know how far I should take the question.

This poet and I haven't spent much time together before this night. His openness surprises me.

He's my brother, the poet says. I love my brother.

Knowing about the rape, I tell him, that must be really hard for you.

My dad, he beat him, the poet says. Really beat him after he found out. Violence with more violence. But I don't think a day goes by that I don't think about what he did. And you want to know the fucked-up thing? The other day, they all went golfing. My brother, the woman he raped, and my dad. I remember how after the rape, there was this whole *boys will be boys* attitude. And now it's been years. So, this guy who assaulted you, he's really open to your project?

Yeah, I tell the poet. He says it's the least he can do.

I was a horny popular guy in high school, the poet says, but I never—I just can't understand why a guy would assault a woman, especially when she's drunk. I remember being drunk with a few buddies in college, and we went into a dorm where a woman was totally naked and passed out on a couch. One of the guys went over and started fingering her, and we all told him to cut it out. It's stupid. It's just so horrible and stupid.

That night, in bed, I wonder about the naked woman. Does she know that a stranger raped her while she was passed out?

I almost wish what Mark wished: that I'd been so drunk I'd forgotten.

...

HIM : But two, the more I think about it, the more I'm certain that some version of what happened was in my head.

M E: You thought that by suggesting—

HIM : That something might happen. I don't think I thought, If I could just get her downstairs I could do this. I'm sure I thought downstairs was to my advantage.

M E: Before I came here, I was talking to my friend Leigh-Anne, a gender studies professor, and I was talking about how the basement really confuses me. There were other parts of the house. The basement stairs were pretty steep as I recall, or maybe not.

HIM : I think they were pretty normal stairs. They're steep if you're drunk.

M E: Being carried down the stairs, I told Leigh-Anne, I keep thinking about that. You're not sure if you suggested the basement?

HIM : I don't remember specifically, but it wouldn't surprise me.

M E: That was the—

HIM : Yeah. I could see that sticking.

M E: Right. Because it's the difference between—

HIM : It's the pivotal—

M E: Right. How premeditated was it?

HIM : Which, I mean—I just—again, I don't know if it's the kind of thing that makes it better or worse, but it honestly wasn't a premeditated decision. It wasn't like I set out at the start of the day.

M E: I haven't been in touch because I've been trying to understand how I feel about all this.

HIM : I mean, I know I said this before, but I kind of assumed we'd never ever talk to one another again—because this thing had happened.

M E: But even recently, I mean. Since the last time we talked. I've been out of touch because I've been trying to figure out my feelings. I went into the project thinking, This will be a fun intellectual exercise because I'm mostly over it.

HIM : Maybe not quite as over it as you thought.

M E: Yeah. I was recently swimming laps and I looked around the pool and no other swimmers were near me, so I went underwater and I screamed—because, you know, I can't let anyone hear me get angry. But yeah, I've felt angry. And I've started remembering more. The night comes back to me at unexpected times. I was telling a friend about this project and she said, Yeah, it's in the zeitgeist. And I wanted to say, That's not why I'm doing it. But then I thought: OK, that is why I'm doing it.

HIM : You can do something that's topical and not have it be because it's topical.

M E: Right. It is something that's been on my mind for a long time now. I told Chris that after Trump got elected I started having nightmares about you and about my newspaper adviser, and Chris told me, It's not since Trump got elected. You've been having those nightmares for as long as we've been together. Every few months, you wake up and I ask you what's wrong and you say, Mark. And I—

HIM : Jesus.

M E: I kind of blocked it. I'd think, Why am I so upset about this thing that wasn't what it—

HIM : I'd rather you be upset with me—

M E: No, I know. [We laugh.]

HIM : Clear enough on that point?

ME: For so long I muddled the narrative, making excuses for you. How you were drunk and all. But then I think about how manipulative you were that night. You hushed me when I started crying, told me that it was just a dream. I recently went through a period where I felt really pissed off. And now, I don't know, fourteen years later, hearing you say that you betrayed me, I feel grateful. And it's so messed up—that I feel grateful to you for acknowledging your betrayal of me and agreeing to all this.

HIM: You can be, but you don't have to be grateful to me.

ME: But that's why I'm interested in the project. Because I can't sort out my feelings. For so long I was afraid to contact you because I worried about your feelings. I didn't want you to get depressed. Chris told me, You can't let Mark's feelings get in the way.

HIM: Chris is a smart guy, it sounds like.

ME: He is. And then I felt so stupid for such a grandiose thought—to think you'd hurt yourself based on this. [We laugh.]

HIM: I laugh because I do the same kind of stuff.

ME: I feel kind of narcissistic there, because why would you hurt yourself because of this? And part of me—what's been helpful is I wanted to know that it affected you, that it wasn't just—

HIM: Yeah, I could see that being useful, to know that remorse existed.

ME: Your apology doesn't seem like an apology crafted by a publicist.

HIM: See, that's what you don't know. I have a team working on my statements. [We laugh.]

ME: The fact that you felt really bad about what happened, that was really helpful for me to know. Not that I wanted it to totally ruin your life.

HIM : But maybe just a little bit?

M E: Well, I am taking power thanks to this project. So maybe I am a passive-aggressive Midwesterner.

HIM : No, that's my job. [We laugh.] We can't both do that.

M E: I mean, this project interests me because it's complicated. The fact that I'm giving you a voice in it—that's going to make a lot of women mad.

HIM : Because I feel like the natural reaction is: I'm supposed to be the irredeemable villain.

M E: The idea of the nice guy, though—

HIM : Nice guys are a total lie.

M E: A lot of times, when I meet a man, any man, I think—at the very start: has this guy raped somebody? I hate that that's my thinking.

HIM : But it's a reality, too.

M E: You mentioned that the assault changed the story you could tell about yourself. What is the story you would tell about yourself?

HIM : I don't know. I don't know how to articulate this.

M E: If you were writing a brief character study of yourself—

HIM : Yeah. I mean, I was a real asshole. Maybe slightly reformed. [Server checks on us.]

M E: Would you have ever expected this?

HIM : Of myself when I was, say, sixteen?

M E: Yeah.

HIM : No. I mean, I think I thought I would have been better than this. And wasn't. Yeah, I think I thought of myself as the exception to most of the rules. In some ways, like I said, the rules didn't apply to me. I used to— it's not comparable—but like, the petty theft. I pirated anything I could get my hands on, just to say that I did, online. I don't know. It was just, after that happened, I don't know. I hated myself for it for a long— [His voice trails off.] I don't know what I'm trying to say.

M E: You mentioned that you'd thought that maybe I was so drunk that I'd forget.

HIM: I almost feel worse about thinking that—

M E: That I'd forget?

HIM: That it would just go away.

M E: But that's an honest answer. I want honest answers. I appreciate your honesty. Is any of this helpful? I wish you well.

HIM: Well, thank you.

M E: You are trying to make it up to me. So that's why I feel able to forgive you. The fact that you agreed. It demonstrates—

HIM: Something. I guess I'm just glad that you're getting something out of it. That part is helpful to me.

M E: I think that some men—usually the perpetrators are men—feel genuine remorse, and some men don't. The ones who don't, sometimes they seem like they feel remorse. They manipulate to get sympathy. But when somebody really seems to feel genuine remorse and tries to make amends, I think it's important to recognise that, to not completely dismiss it. It's like with prisoners.

HIM: This project is my rehabilitation. [We laugh.]

M E: I'm not saying we shouldn't punish men—again, they're usually men—for sexual assault. I'm worried that a strain of conservative thinking is entering modern feminism. This zero-tolerance policy: no matter what, he's banished. Away with him.

HIM: He is a bad guy and we put him in a warehouse for fifty years.

M E: And I don't think that's always productive for society.

HIM: I'm not, in general, interested in zero-tolerance policies.

M E: One thing I found hard when writing my first book: I thought of us as close friends, but the only appearance of you—

HIM: Well, to be in the book for more than that—I mean, it's a book about your dad. It's a book about a lot of things.

M E: As a writer, you have to make decisions. You can't include everything. But you also can't force the narrative into some tidy plot. And that's why this project, why it's so complicated. Like I said, I'm also writing about my good memories of us. You were a supportive friend.

HIM: I'm happy you can still think of me in that way. That it didn't completely crowd out all of those memories. Because it did for me for a long time.

M E: Crowd out the good memories?

HIM: For a long, long time, it had sort of shrunk down our relationship to just: we were friends and then I did this horrible thing and then, the end.

M E: It scared me when you couldn't send me five good memories right away. I worried I'd misconstrued the friendship. But overall, it's been really helpful to me, this project. How are you feeling about it?

HIM: Anxious. But I'm anxious about everything.

M E: Is there anything I haven't asked that you think we should discuss?

HIM: I feel like you've been pretty thorough.

M E: I'm just now remembering one of the questions that I left back at the hotel: after our first conversation, where did you see this going? This relationship going.

HIM: I really wasn't sure. To be honest, part of me was just glad to hear from you. And then, I felt—I felt—I spent about the three or four days leading up to that first phone call just in full-blown existential dread. And then I was just kind of distraught afterwards. Which I think I sent a couple pictures. But—I don't know. I was really not sure where it was going after that first phone call. And I was very nervous about it. I felt quite a bit better after our second phone call, which I felt like we were able to hit more on how you were feeling about it. [Server brings check and I grab it.] Do you want to split it?

M E: No. I ordered more drinks than you did. I'll get it. You can get tomorrow.

HIM : OK. I feel like I win that deal. [We laugh.]

M E: So you felt better after the second phone call.

HIM : Yeah, and part of that was just—because I had been up, either the night before or the day before—I had read your book in one sitting.

M E: Selfish question: did you read the print copy or the Kindle?

HIM : The print copy.

M E: OK, good. [We laugh.]

HIM : I'm not an animal. [We laugh.]

M E: OK, that makes me feel better. That's actually been on my mind. But it's one of those questions—

HIM : That you feel ridiculous asking. [We laugh.]

M E: Yeah. Because the formatting is slightly off at times in the Kindle—like, there's not enough white space between the chapter openings, those sort of meta sections, and the chapters themselves. And anyway, print books, they're such a better experience.

HIM : But yeah, I had read it in one sitting, shortly before we spoke. So I was not in a particularly good place. Which is fine. I feel like I keep saying stuff and then I have no idea where I'm going with it.

M E: That's OK. We're talking about a hard subject. [Server takes credit card.] Where do you see things going now?

HIM : I don't know. It's kind of like you said: friendship between men and women is hard in the best of circumstances. Obviously, we're never going to be in a relationship. I would like to stay in contact, but also I'm bad at that.

M E: I have a few close male friends. But when you and I became friends, we were so young. [Server brings back receipt for me to sign.] What was I saying? I don't remember. Oh, but yeah, friendships. I don't think it's impossible for men and women to be friends. It is hard to—sorry, I need to figure out the math here.

HIM: So as not to accidentally tip her two dollars?

M E: I tend to overtip out of a fear of undertipping. My bank has called me on multiple occasions to ask: did you mean to leave a forty percent tip? [We laugh.] Do you think participating in this has changed any of your approaches to—do you think you'll make any changes? [Server comes back, takes receipt.] I think they really want us to go. [We laugh.]

HIM: Since she's over here every three minutes. Maybe we should leave and talk outside.

M E: OK.

HIM: Is it obnoxious to say that I think of myself as a feminist?

M E: No. I don't think so.

HIM: Or at least attempt to be?

M E: But I mean, do you think your friendships—

HIM: I don't know. If you're asking, Do you think this handful of conversations is going to be the miracle cure and I'm going to have the normal happy life? I don't realistically see that. But it's been good. To get some of this out in the open.

M E: Do you think you'll talk about it with anyone else?

HIM: I seriously doubt it. I mean, where do you start with something like that?

M E: Therapy? [We laugh.]

HIM: I guess. But how do you start that conversation? You're in a slightly different position in that regard. I did this awful thing to you. Who wants to hear about my side of I-did-this-really-awful-thing?

M E: For enough money, a therapist would— [We laugh.]

HIM : Yeah, for a couple hundred bucks an hour.

M E: I told my therapist, Maybe I should look up therapists for Mark. And my therapist said, No. No. Mark can go do that. And I said, Maybe there's sliding-scale. And he said, It's not your job to find him therapy.

HIM : You're trying to fix things.

M E: Yeah, I guess so.

HIM : I'm comfortable being broken.

M E: OK. Let's head out. Let me stop this. I have this fear that it didn't record any of this.

EVENTUALLY, I'LL JUST STOP THINKING OF HIM

I draft a list of post-Mark-conversation resolutions:

1. stop letting men talk over me,
2. disagree vocally when I disagree mentally,
3. stop volunteering to do more.

I meet with Jung and Molly at the restaurant where we usually meet to discuss our writing.

The last conversation I had with Mark, I tell them, he said that his parents would be really happy to hear from me. That's strange, right? I think it'd drive me nuts to say hello to his parents and not explain why I disappeared.

Maybe he wants to get caught, Jung says.

Or, maybe, Molly says, he actually believes that you'll keep what he did a secret.

If I get in touch with his parents, I say, and pretend as if the rape didn't happen—for me to behave as if it never happened, it tells Mark that he can pretend it never happened.

I'm impressed, Jung says, that you're able to stay focused on this. I'd be too angry.

I feel sort of angry, I say. But it's as if I can't hold on to it for long enough. I think the project is actually getting in the way of that.

Walking back to my house from the restaurant, I think that if the guy who raped me in New York photographed an abandoned factory to demonstrate, to me, his tortured conscience over raping me, I'd be annoyed. Angry, in fact. Furious. But because I'm constantly thinking about plot elements and metaphors for this book, his photographs become useful—to the project, anyway. Processing my feelings is hard to do authentically—because the project, the thing I intended to get at the truth, is getting in my way of understanding my feelings. And writing about this material, I feel compelled to turn off my emotions so as to remain focused.

But this book also gives me some sense of control. I can take charge of the material. I can include and cut what I want.

As if reading my thoughts today, Mark shares photos that he took from a hot-air balloon. He explains in a text: *My mom wanted to go on a hot-air balloon ride because it was a bucket list thing for her, so I tagged along and took these. It was kind of a fun challenge to visualise shots in real time because obviously you don't have any control over where you're going, so you can't chase perfect frames too much.*

So, we went from an abandoned factory to a hot-air balloon? I take it he's feeling better. I put on the mood ring and agree with its conclusion: I feel unsettled mixed emotions.

I email Mark a release form. The publisher needs it, I explain. Mark signs it and emails it back within a few hours. He doesn't ask to read the manuscript.

We arrange to talk this weekend. But then a few hours later, he cancels. He's not feeling well. I don't really need to talk with him.

But I want to know: will he ever tell his parents?

If Mark tells them that he raped me, then maybe I really could move on. I like to think that someday he will tell them. He'll hand this book to them and say, Mark is me. And they'll read it and understand why I disappeared from their lives.

Instead of describing to my mom what Mark did, I'll hand her the finished manuscript—because how do I even begin that conversation?

The semester starts in a week. I'd like to spend my remaining summer days—the next year, really—revising this manuscript, teasing it apart, sentence by sentence, ensuring the stressed syllables outnumber the unstressed, stuff like that. But the temptation to censor my thoughts and feelings in the revision process is too strong. So instead of revising what's here, I revise my Writing Creative Non-fiction syllabus. I add a section about sexual assault resources.

I text Mark again, ask if he can talk. He replies. He says yes.

I skim the transcripts and realise I never asked him if he'd been sexually assaulted. How did I miss that?

So I call him, one last time.

. . .

M E: You said that your parents and siblings would be really happy to hear from me. The idea of my reaching out to them. I'm curious to know where you think that impulse comes from.

HIM : I think it's that we were all friends, and my parents loved you. They loved all my friends. And that doesn't really go away. As much as it's counter to my interest of not having to live with this with the rest of my family, they would, I'm sure, love to hear from you.

M E: Do you see how that would be hard for me?

HIM : Right. I guess there's an element of, Is he not getting it?

M E: Yeah, that is what I've been thinking. Also, I've been wondering if—does some part of you want to get caught? Because you've said that it feels good to get a lot of this off your chest. And when you said that it would destroy your relationship with your dad, part of me—I didn't say this at the time, but part of me didn't, doesn't, think it would. A lot of parents love their kids regardless. You see the parents of murderers still support their kids.

HIM : You've got a point there. They would still love me. But it would irrevocably alter our relationship as opposed to destroy it.

M E: OK, and then the other part of me, the one operating under the assumption that you don't want to get caught, that part of me thought, It's strange that he thinks I would be able to have a conversation with his parents—I don't know. That I could compartmentalise in that way. Because I couldn't. That's why I fell out of touch with them. And I can't—I can't imagine having a conversation with them.

HIM : Yeah. I guess we're a family of not really talking about the things that are bothering us. You internalise that. Our whole family dynamic is piles of passive aggression.

M E: You know, I had a nightmare about this the other day. I was at your house. I was in the front room with your parents, and you were watching me talk with them, and they were asking me what I was working on, and I felt awkward. I lied, said I was writing poetry, and you looked happy, and, I don't know. I understand recounting one's dream can be pretty boring for the listener, but whatever. [We laugh.] I love hearing people's dreams. So anyway. I went for a tour through your house and the rooms had been moved around. But my most vivid memory of the nightmare is how happy you looked, and how uncomfortable I felt. Talking with your parents took so much effort. And, OK, going back to our conversation at the café, you mentioned that you don't think your mom would hold it against me now. And I've told you, several times now, that I feel really bad about falling out of touch with them. I've been afraid that they held it against me—because I just kind of disappeared.

HIM : But I mean that happens. It's happened to most of my high school friends.

M E: But I would have rather disappeared for some other reason. So when you mentioned that you didn't think your mom would hold it against me now—did she hold it against me?

HIM : Not that she ever said to me. I don't think she has any ill feelings toward you. I mean, I'm sure she would have taken my sister's side in whatever dispute you two had.

M E: Right. The thing about the Fulbright fellowship.

HIM : I mean, God, it was what? Fifteen years ago?

M E: I just wonder, if Amber really told your sister what had happened, like you said, then is that partly why your sister ended her friendship with me? Was it too hard for her to acknowledge what you did to me? It was so weird. She cut me off because I suggested she apply for a Fulbright teaching fellowship?

HIM : That is a line of reasoning that is totally in keeping with my sister. I'm willing to believe that it's just that. She's always been hyper-defensive about intelligence and achievement and stuff. I think she's sometimes felt pressured to be more academic than she feels comfortable being.

M E: OK. Well, the main reason I called was to follow up on your suggestions to reach out to your parents and siblings. To ask your sister what she knows.

HIM : I guess the other part of that, there's some of—
I've been trying to be conscious of not attempting
to control what you're doing with this project. To my
mind, if you needed to talk to my sister—

M E: I was surprised that you'd think I could reach out to
any of them. That is the thing that's been really hard for
me. I didn't like disappearing. It was really hard to never
talk to your family again.

HIM : Yeah. It's an understandable act of self-preservation
at that point.

M E: Partly, yeah, it was self-preservation. But also, I was
afraid of seeing them and crying and then it coming
out, what had happened. Really, I was protecting you.
It sounds like you don't think you would ever tell them.

HIM : I mean, I can't say I'm planning on it.

M E: I'm not asking you to. I just wasn't sure how to read
the suggestion, which is why I'm following up on it. And
OK, and now another big question that I thought I had
asked you: have you ever been sexually assaulted? Did I
ever ask you that?

HIM : You haven't asked me. But if you're curious, no, I
have not been.

M E: OK, it was one of those questions that I thought
to ask you way back and apparently just never did. OK,
so those were the big questions, really big questions I
recognise, that I wanted to ask you.

HIM : No, it's fine. The general thrust of this, it's
possibly sociopathic, the extent to which you are
compartmentalising things is not alien to me. [We
laugh.]

M E: Entering writer mode, that's given me some control
and allowed me to not think about a lot of this.

HIM : I mean, it's going to be easier for me than it is for
you on this subject.

M E: I still haven't told my mom what I'm working on.

HIM : That's got to be tough too. To not know how to talk about it with her.

M E: Does some part of you actually want your parents to know what happened?

HIM : I mean, yeah, I don't think you're wrong there in that. There is a part of me that wishes I could have that conversation in a way that isn't selfish and destructive. But I don't see any good coming from it.

M E: That it would just hurt them.

HIM : Yeah.

M E: Well, if you ever decide to tell them, perhaps the book is an easier way to do that.

HIM : Yeah, I'll just buy my mom a copy of the book for Christmas. [We laugh.] Look what Jeannie wrote. [We laugh.]

M E: I was thinking about how you mentioned that your dad was very conscientiously ethical and always cares about doing the right thing by people, and I was wondering if that was motivating you with this project.

HIM : Yeah, I mean there would be a degree of contempt involved that I'm not eager to pursue.

M E: What do you mean?

HIM : I think I would basically lose my dad's respect.

M E: Oh, if you didn't participate.

HIM : No, if I told him what, what had happened.

M E: Oh, OK. What I mean is, what you're doing, talking with me, it's the ethical thing to do.

HIM : I don't think that would be the aspect of that conversation that would be most relevant to him.

M E: One more question. Do you think you'll date? Or is that not of interest to you?

HIM : It's not that it's not of interest to me, but the longer it's gone on where—how do you go out on a first date and say, I'm a thirty-four-year-old man and I've never—I've never done this or that or the other thing?

So, I don't know. We'll see what happens. And then, you know, I don't know if you can say it's depression-related or fatigue-related, but I get home from work and I don't want to be around people.

M E: How have you been doing?

HIM: I'm not depressed or anything. I just legitimately had—I don't know if it was a cold or allergies or some hellish combination of both, but I was sick. I wasn't ducking your call last weekend. I know how it looks. I legitimately had a migraine and then a fever since yesterday.

M E: I didn't think you were lying about being sick. But I guess I was concerned that you were maybe depressed. And there I go. I slip into this, How are you feeling? I don't want to upset you. Actually, I've been really annoyed by myself in looking over the transcripts—because, within, I think within a page I said: I hope you know I don't hate you, I hope you know I think you're a really good person, I hope this is somewhat helpful to you. [We laugh.] It's absurd. It's embarrassing. I didn't know I did it that much. There's part of me that would love to remove all that. [We laugh.]

HIM: It's endearing in a way. You could do a deep dive on why is that your default reaction.

M E: It's absurd how much I do it.

HIM: Spending half of the conversation propping me up.

M E: Yeah! [We laugh.] I praise you a lot. You're kind of good at everything: things like that. What's weird, though, I was feeling when we last met, there was a way in which that because we were friends, I wondered, Do I hug him?

HIM: The whole thing is, I'm going to reuse the word, fraught.

M E: It's been an interesting experience trying to do this. So thank you. It's weird to thank you for this, but thank you.

HIM : You realise you're doing it again, right?

M E: I know. [We laugh.]

HIM : The nice thing is, you get to decide what goes in the book.

M E: I do.

THIS IS WHERE WE ARE

Last night, I had another nightmare about Mark. So much for resolution.

Today is the first day of class. After I briefly review the syllabus with my students, one of them asks me, If someone writes about being raped but doesn't want it reported, then she shouldn't say that it happened on campus or that another student committed the rape. Is that right?

This is where we are.

I return to Hannah's essay, to the sentence I suggested cutting: *A grown woman, now—or growing still—who has survived so much and still has so much to survive.*
  I regret my suggestion. I want that line.

Resources for Victims of Domestic Violence, Sexual Assault and Rape

How to report a rape or sexual assault: call 999 as soon as possible after the crime. For more information, visit:
www.gov.uk/report-rape-sexual-assault

ENGLAND AND WALES

Rape Crisis Centres: provides specialist support and services to women and girls who have experienced rape, sexual violence, or sexual abuse at any time. www.rapecrisis.org.uk

Victim Support: provides emotional support and practical help to victims of all crimes, including rape and sexual assault, whether or not it has been reported to the police.
24/7 Supportline: 0808 16 89 111 – www.victimsupport.org.uk

Support for domestic violence and sexual assault:
www.uksaysnomore.org/get-help/ – https://www.hestia.org/brightsky

The Survivors Trust: supports and empowers survivors of rape, sexual violence and/or childhood sexual abuse
www.thesurvivorstrust.org – 0808 801 0818

Safeline: a charity working to prevent sexual abuse and to support those affected in their recovery. – www.safeline.org.uk

SCOTLAND

Rape Crisis Scotland: www.rapecrisisscotland.org.uk

Rape and sexual assault support: www.mygov.scot/rape-assault/

NORTHERN IRELAND

24 Hour Domestic and Sexual Abuse Helpline:
0808 802 1414 – help@dsahelpline.org – www.dsahelpline.org

IRELAND

Information about professional support and choices available to survivors of sexual violence.
www.rapecrisishelp.ie - 24 Hour Helpline on 1800 778888